Carson-Dellosa Publishing

Four-Blocks® Plan Book "Plus"

The Four-Blocks® Literacy Model

Grades 1-3

GUIDED READING

SELF-SELECTED READING

WRITING

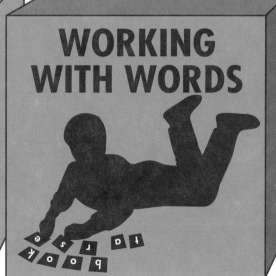

WORKING WITH WORDS

Compiled by and Additional Activities Provided by
Joyce Kohfeldt
I.E.S.S., Inc., Kernersville, NC

Illustrator
Kathryn Mitter

Art Adaptations
Pam Thayer

Editor
Tracy Soles

"**J**ust as all children do not learn in the same way, all teachers do not plan lessons in the same way! The *Four-Blocks® Plan Book "Plus"* remains true to the Four-Blocks® Literacy Model, yet offers teachers the flexibility they need in order to personalize their daily lesson plans."

Patricia M Cunningham

Dorothy P. Hall

Cheryl M. Sigmon

D1405266

TABLE OF CONTENTS

How To Use This Plan Book

This plan book was designed to meet the needs of first-, second-, and third-grade teachers who are currently using the Four-Blocks® Literacy Model as well as the needs of teachers who are just beginning to implement the model in their classrooms. This versatile tool combines many popular elements of typical plan books with additional features specific to the Four-Blocks® Literacy Model, allowing you to plan weekly lessons for all the subjects you teach.

Standard Plan Book Features:

- **Class Roster (pages 6-7)**

  Record student and parent names, along with addresses, phone numbers, fax and e-mail numbers, student bus assignments, and student birthdays. Use the notes area to list any special needs a student may have, such as necessary medication, etc.

- **Room Arrangement (page 10)**

  Customize your seating arrangement to match the needs of your students, the size of your classroom, and your preferred teaching style. Use the blank space on page 10 to sketch out your ideas. To make this page reusable, cover the blank area with clear contact paper. Then, use grease pencils, erasable markers, or overhead markers to draw your room arrangement. Changes to your room layout can easily be recorded by simply erasing and redrawing. Helpful Hint: Use small sticky notes to finalize the room arrangement before drawing it on the page. Write each student's name on a sticky note, along with the names of other classroom furniture and objects, such as the pocket chart stand, your desk, student cubbies, etc. Reposition the sticky notes until you find an arrangement that works, then transfer the final arrangement to the page.

- **Substitute Information (page 11)**

  Be sure to update Substitute Information periodically throughout the school year. You may also wish to make a copy of this completed page for your school secretary or assistant to keep on hand. Place a note on your desk telling where the substitute information can be found in case of an unexpected absence.

- **Long-Term Planning (page 111)**

  Some items/events you may wish to record on the long-term planning page include special themes or units, dates of parent/teacher conferences, deadlines for forms or evaluations, convention or inservice dates, dates for standardized testing, etc.

- **Reproducible Parent Contact Record (page 110)**

  Record your contact with students' parents, whether by phone call, e-mail, fax, note home, or conference. This form includes space for detailed notes on the purpose of the contact, what was said, and any follow-up actions that are necessary.

Special Four-Blocks Features:

- **How Does a Four-Blocks Classroom Look? (pages 8-9)**

  Text and illustrations provide a glimpse into a Four-Blocks classroom. Use the tips given on these pages to help create your own room arrangement.

- **Four-Blocks Summaries and Checklists (pages 12-15)**

  A summary of each of the Four Blocks, along with the time frame for each segment within the block, will provide helpful reminders when planning activities or sharing information with parents and students. The teacher checklists allow you to self-monitor the implementation of each block. The checklists would also help administrators know what criteria to look for when observing in Four-Blocks classrooms.

- **Planning Pages (pages 16-93)**

  Thirty-nine weeks of planning pages are provided in this plan book. Sample planning pages are provided on pages 4-5 to show how a full week's lesson plans might look. Use the open design of the pages for flexible planning by drawing your own vertical lines where needed. Dotted guidelines at one-inch intervals have been added to make it easier for you. There's plenty of space for lesson plans in math, science, social studies, etc. Along the right side of each two-page planning week, the Four-Blocks Weekly Record provides space for easy daily recording of your Four-Blocks activities, reading materials, and serves as a reminder of your daily schedule. The "Special Events This Week" space along the bottom of the page can be used to write reminders of appointments, conferences, special assemblies, etc.

- **Activities for Each Block (pages 94-110)**

  This section of the plan book includes brief instructions for activities within each of the Four Blocks. In addition, this section also includes reproducibles for student and teacher use, such as:

  Reading Conference questions (page 94)
  Balance in Book Baskets (page 95)
  Bookmarks (page 96)
  Reproducible Graphic Organizers (pages 98-99)
  Reproducible Editing Checklist (page 103)
  Writing Conferences Checklist (page 104)
  Word Wall word lists for first, second, and third grades (page 106)
  Making Words lessons (page 107)
  Guess the Covered Word lessons for first, second, and third grades (page 108)
  Changing a Hen to a Fox (page 108)
  Tongue Twisters (page 110)

Monday	8:30-8:50 Opening	8:50-9:30 Guided Reading Spiders (¹/₂) Before: Picture Walk / Begin KWL / During: Partners Read/ Sticky Notes / After: Add to KWL	9:30-10:00 Working w/Words Word Wall: Add 5 new words / Reading/Writing Rhymes w/ spelling pattern "__at"	10:00-10:30 P. E.	10:30-11:15 Math Subtraction (counters) (See pages 12-13 in math book)	11:20-12:00 Lunch/Recess	12:00-12:40 Writing Mini-lesson: Choosing a topic (Spiders) / Conferences w/ students / Author's Chair
Tuesday	Opening / Jake's birthday	Guided Reading Spiders (finish) Before: Review info on KWL / During: Partners Read/ Sticky Notes / After: Finish KWL	Working w/ Words / Word Wall: Review 5 new words / Making Words (spider)	Music	Math Review addition and subtraction See pages 14-17 in book (no counters)	Lunch/Recess	Writing Mini-lesson: Adding on to a piece / Conferences w/ students / Author's Chair
Wednesday	Opening / Parent Reader (Tony M.'s dad)	Guided Reading Alexander Who Used To Be Rich Last Sunday Before: Preview/Predictions / During: Partners Read / After: Discussion (use Beach Ball*)	Working w/ Words / Word Wall: Review 5 new words / On-the-Back: Rhyming Words (line, fine, mine, nine, twine, spine, etc.) / Guess the Covered Word	Art	Math Adding and subtracting money up to $1.00 See pages 21-22 (connect to Alexander Who Used To Be Rich Last Sunday)	Lunch/Recess	Writing Mini-lesson: Using WW and Editing Checklist: ◯ questionable words / Conferences w/ students / Author's Chair
Thursday	Opening	Guided Reading Alexander Who Used To Be Rich Last Sunday Before: Begin story map / During: 3-Ring Circus* / After: Complete story map	Working w/ Words / Word Wall: Review any 5 words / On-the-Back: Endings / Rounding Up the Rhymes w/ My Sister Ate One Hare	Computers	Math Adding and subtracting money (1's, 10's, and 100's) See pages 23-25	Lunch/Recess	Writing Mini-lesson: Editing Checklist– capitals / Conferences w/ students / Author's Chair
Friday	Opening / Collect field trip money.	Guided Reading Before: Sequence of Events for "play" / During: Read individually/ Teacher w/ groups / After: Review sequence "Doing" the Book	Working w/ Words / Word Wall: Review any 5 words w/ Be A Mind Reader / Changing a Hen to a Fox	Library	Math Money Equivalents (up to $1.00) overhead coins and small groups (4) Using coins "cover up" game	Lunch/Recess	Writing Mini-lesson: Staying on topic / Conferences w/ students / Author's Chair

Special Events This Week:

Monday p.m. – Bus duty   Tuesday – Jake's birthday   Thursday – Dentist appointment at 4:30

*For more information, see *The Teacher's Guide to the Four Blocks®*.

12:45–1:30 Science/Art	1:30–2:10 Self-Selected Reading	2:15–2:45 Centers	2:45–3:00
Science: Spiders and their webs (text pp. 18–24) Art: Creating spider webs	Read aloud: An informational book about spiders Talk about reading pictures Children read	Small group—Jake, Shelley, Billy, and LaDawn (extra reading strategies)	Daily wrap-up
Science: Video Spiders and Webs (See science book text on pages 25–29) Discussion: Comparing six different examples	Self-Selected Reading Read aloud: Spiders (harder read than one used in Monday's Guided Reading; has many photos) Children read	Centers Help in Math Center	Daily wrap-up Jake's party
Science: Venn Diagram w/ 2 spiders Focus: Characteristics of spiders (alike, different) ⚭ Art: Paint your favorite spider	Self-Selected Reading Read aloud: Another Alexander book by Judith Viorst Children read	Centers Small group (extra reading for Karen, Carlos, Doris)	Daily wrap-up
Social Studies: Communities Whole class web for communities	Self-Selected Reading Read aloud: Counting Crocodiles Children read	Centers Help in Art Center	Daily wrap-up
Social Studies: Communities Discuss part of web "community helpers" Art: Draw a picture of a community helper Write a sentence about a community helper (if time)	Self-Selected Reading Read aloud: Another Judith Viorst book Talk about the author we are reading Children read	Centers Small group (extra reading for Antoine, Tony S., Shelby)	Daily wrap-up

☐ Guided Reading ⏱ 30-40 min.

Before (5-10 min.)
During (15-20 min.)
After (5-10 min.)

M	Before	Picture Walk/KWL
	During	Partners Read
	After	Begin L of KWL
T	Before	KWL
	During	Partners Read
	After	Complete KWL
W	Before	Preview/Predictions
	During	Partners Read
	After	Discussion
Th	Before	Begin Story Map
	During	3-Ring Circus
	After	Complete Story Map
F	Before	Sequence of Events
	During	Indv. Reading/Teacher w/ groups
	After	"Doing" the Book

☐ Self-Selected Reading ⏱ 30-40 min.

Teacher Read-Aloud (5-10 min.)

M	Informational book on spiders
T	Spiders
W	Another Alexander book
Th	Counting Crocodiles
F	Another Judith Viorst book

Reading Conferences (15-20 min.)

M	José, Mike, Betty, Anna, Jerome
T	Jake, Rachel, Juan, Tony M.
W	Alex, Karen, Carlos, Shelby, Bill
Th	Joe, Tony S., Janet, Sue
F	Thomas, Sandy, Antoine, Peggy, Doris, Bobby

Sharing (5-10 min.)

M	Betty, Jerome, Alex
T	José, Tony S.
W	Shelby, Bill
Th	Jake, Janet
F	Doris, Antoine, Rachel

☐ Writing ⏱ 30-40 min.

Mini-Lesson (5-10 min.)

M	Choosing a topic
T	Adding on to a piece
W	Using Word Wall
Th	Editing-capitals (◯ words/spelling)
F	Staying on topic

Writing/Conferences (15-20 min.)

M	Jake, Sam, Juan
T	Tony M., Alex, Karen
W	Shelby, Doris, Bobby
Th	Bill, Janet, Sue
F	Thomas, José, Mike

Sharing-Author's Chair (5-10 min.)

M	Joey, Anna, Jerome
T	Mike, Antoine
W	Rachel, Carlos
Th	Doris, Betty
F	Sandy, Tony S.

☐ Working with Words ⏱ 30 min.

Word Wall Words (10 min.)

because	eating
line	outside
people	

On-The-Back Activity (see page 105)

M	
T	
W	Rhyming Words (line, mine, etc.)
Th	Endings
F	Be A Mind Reader

Words Activity (20 min.)
(Circle appropriate day)

M Ⓣ W Th F	Making Words (spider)
M T Ⓦ Th F	Guess the Covered Word
M T W Th F	Using Words You Know
M T W Ⓣⓗ F	Rounding Up the Rhymes
Ⓜ T W Th F	Reading/Writing Rhymes (_at)
M T W Th Ⓕ	Other Changing a Hen to a Fox

Class Roster

Student Name	Parent/Guardian Names	Address

HOME PHONE	WORK PHONE	FAX/E-MAIL	BUS ASSIGNMENT	BIRTHDAY	NOTES

How Does A Four-Blocks Classroom Look?

As you look into the classroom, you are likely to see...

- Desks or tables arranged in groups of four, in U-shapes, etc., so that students can work in cooperative groups.

- A Word Wall with letters of the alphabet stretching across a wall and words written on colored paper and organized under the appropriate letter of the alphabet.

- A pocket chart readily available for a number of activities, such as Making Words and Rounding Up the Rhymes.

- Student work displayed in the room—compositions on bulletin boards, student and class-made books on shelves and tables, artwork decorating the walls, etc.

- Charts with vocabulary words clustered by theme or topic. These are words that are valuable for students to learn, but which may not be appropriate for the Word Wall.

- An Editor's Checklist written on large chart paper or poster board to be used as a reference for writers as they complete their quick editing on rough drafts.

- Books, books, and more books placed in baskets for Self-Selected Reading, displayed attractively on shelves and window sills, in a class library area, and in other places around the room.

- Other reading materials such as magazines, newspapers, and resource materials placed where students can easily access them.

- Samples of environmental print, such as news clippings, signs, cereal boxes, and other packaging, that show evidence that reading has real-world applications.

- Writing materials in a center or area of the room for students' use. The center will include writing paper in various colors and shapes, stationery and postcards, a stapler, construction paper, glue, crayons, pens, pencils, and perhaps one or two computers for composing.

- A carpeted area or rug where students gather close to the teacher for mini-lessons and read-alouds.

- An inexpensive kitchen timer used by the teacher to assure brisk pacing of each of the Four-Blocks.

- Teachers and students engaged in teaching and learning.

Information appears in *Implementing the 4-Blocks® Model.*

A Glance at a Four-Blocks Classroom

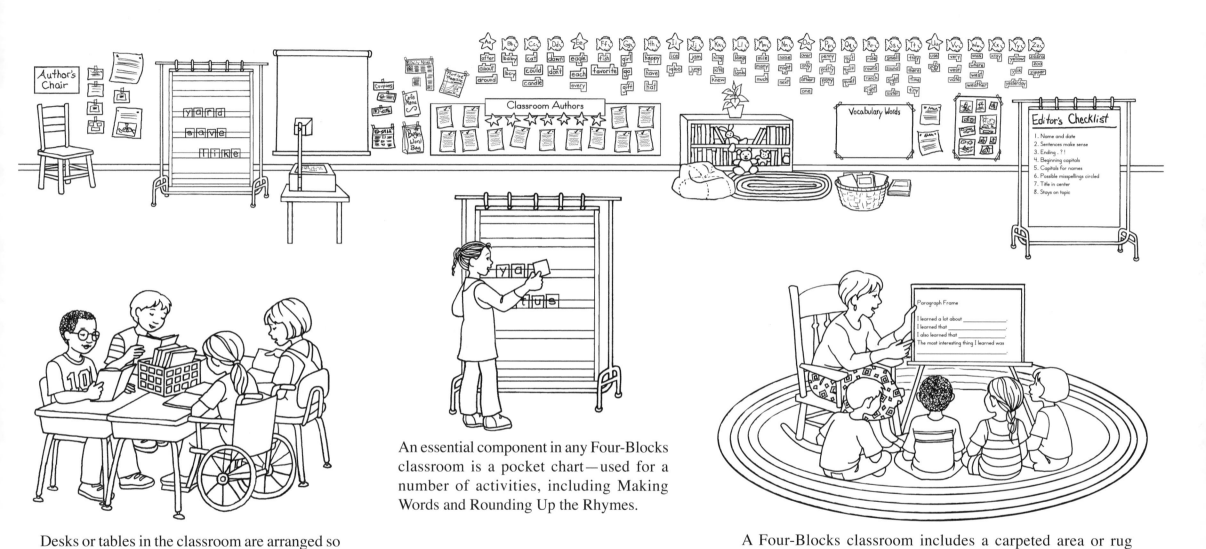

An essential component in any Four-Blocks classroom is a pocket chart—used for a number of activities, including Making Words and Rounding Up the Rhymes.

Desks or tables in the classroom are arranged so that students can work in cooperative groups and usually include "book baskets" which contain various types of reading materials.

A Four-Blocks classroom includes a carpeted area or rug where students gather close to the teacher for mini-lessons, read-alouds, and other small group activities.

(This is a partial classroom scene.)

ROOM ARRANGEMENT

Your room arrangement will largely depend on the size and shape of your classroom, how much interaction you wish for students to have with each other, and your basic teaching philosophy. (For more information on how a Four-Blocks classroom should look, please refer to pages 8-9.) Whatever seating plan you choose, be sure to have an area where you and your students can gather for read-alouds, mini-lessons, and other group activities. Of course, you should be able to see all of the students and all of the students should be able to see you, the chalkboard, the Word Wall, and other important elements in the room. Use the space below to diagram your room arrangement.

SUBSTITUTE INFORMATION

DAILY SCHEDULE

Opening

Lunch

Dismissal

Recess
  Outdoor
    Time
    Area
  Indoor
    Time
    Area
Rainy Day Activities

STUDENTS WITH SPECIAL CLASSES

Name	Class	Day/Time

SPECIAL SCHEDULES

Day/Time	Duties

SPECIAL CLASSES

Subject	Teacher	Day/Time	Room
Art			
Gym			
Computers			
Music			
Library			
Other			

MATERIAL/EQUIPMENT LOCATION

For help, please see...

EMERGENCY PROCEDURES

Fire Drill

Storm Drill

MISCELLANEOUS

If you need help, ask...

Helpful Teachers

Helpful Students

Principal

Custodian

Other

NOTES FOR THE SUBSTITUTE

Summary of the
Self-Selected Reading Block

Purpose: To build fluency in reading, to allow students to read and enjoy text that is appropriate to their own independent reading levels, and to build confidence in students as readers.

Total Time: 30 - 40 minutes

Segment One: Teacher Read-Aloud

5-10 min.

The teacher reads aloud to all students from a variety of genres, topics, and authors.

Segment Two: Independent Reading and Conferencing

15-20 min.

1. Students move to a reading area and select a book, or choose a book or magazine from the basket at their table to read independently.

2. The teacher holds conferences with 3-5 children daily as the other children read. She keeps a conference form recording each child's individual progress, preferences, and responses.

Segment Three (Optional): Sharing

5-10 min.

1. Several students share briefly (approximately two minutes each) with the whole class what they have read.

2. If time allows, the reader answers several questions from classmates about the book. The teacher models the types of thoughtful questions children should ask.

Teacher's Checklist for
Self-Selected Reading

In preparing and presenting my lesson in this block, I have...

_____ 1. Provided a good model of fluency in reading and attempted to motivate students through a teacher read-aloud daily. My read-aloud was clear, expressive, and enthusiastic.

_____ 2. Provided an adequate supply of books and other reading materials on various topics, of different genres, and on varied reading levels (above, below, and on grade level).

_____ 3. Made books easily accessible to children so that they will not lose time in choosing and trading books.

_____ 4. Divided the class so that I know which days I will have conferences with each child.

_____ 5. Limited the time spent on each conference to 3–5 minutes.

_____ 6. Used questions in my conferences that let children know what is important about their reading rather than emphasizing minor details.

_____ 7. Guided and encouraged children during the conference to read books on appropriate levels, while still allowing freedom of choice.

_____ 8. Promoted reading through teacher read-alouds and book talks at several appropriate times throughout the day

_____ 9. Connected read-alouds, when possible, to a subject, theme, or concept which the class has studied or will study.

Please refer to pages 94-96 for additional information, ideas, and activities for the Self-Selected Reading Block.

Information appears in *The Teacher's Guide to the Four Blocks®* and *Implementing the 4-Blocks® Model*.

SUMMARY OF THE GUIDED READING BLOCK

Purpose: To build comprehension and fluency with reading, and to introduce students to a variety of literature, such as stories, informational text, and poetry.

Total Time: 30 - 40 minutes

5-10 min.

Segment One: Before Reading

1. The teacher introduces and supports grade-level and easier text in a number of ways over multiple days:
   - building on students' prior knowledge about the text and topic.
   - beginning graphic organizers, such as webs and story maps.
   - guiding picture discussion and prediction.
   - discussing key vocabulary in context.
2. The teacher focuses the lesson on a comprehension skill or strategy.

15-20 min.

Segment Two: Reading

1. The teacher provides flexible grouping of all students to read the text. Grouping may be paired (partner), individual, small groups reading with the teacher, three-ring circus, or Book Club Groups and can include special teachers or volunteers.
2. The children read the selections. The teacher listens to children reading, coaching those who need help and sometimes taking anecdotal notes.

5-10 min.

Segment Three: After Reading

The teacher directs the whole group in closure activities to match the purpose. These activities may include the following:
   - discussion of text/literature.
   - acting out the story.
   - writing in response to reading.
   - completion of a graphic organizer.
   - discussion of the skill or strategy introduced in Segment One.

TEACHER'S CHECKLIST FOR GUIDED READING

In preparing and presenting my lesson in this block, I have...

_____ 1. Presented a comprehension skill or strategy before reading and followed it up after reading.

_____ 2. Introduced new material by previewing pictures and making predictions.

_____ 3. Provided grade level and easier material for this block.

_____ 4. Used basals, copies of trade books, big books, and content area materials.

_____ 5. Established prior knowledge by helping students make connections between the content and what is familiar to them.

_____ 6. Varied the types of materials/texts presented on multiple days during this block.

_____ 7. Established and stated a clear purpose for students' reading and followed this up after reading.

_____ 8. Provided consistent models of the types of higher-level questions that students should ask of themselves, partners, and literacy circles during and after reading.

_____ 9. Arranged grouping during Segment Two (Reading) that is flexible and purposeful. Readers who need greater levels of support are paired with stronger readers or work in a small group. No grouping remains stagnant or easily identifiable, especially with struggling readers.

Please refer to pages 97-101 for additional information, ideas, and activities for the Guided Reading Block.

Information appears in *The Teacher's Guide to the Four Blocks®* and *Implementing the 4-Blocks® Model.*

SUMMARY OF THE WRITING BLOCK

Purpose: To build fluency in writing, to apply the writing process, to refine and apply knowledge of phonics, and to build students' confidence as writers.

Total Time: 30 - 40 minutes

5-10 min.

Segment One: Mini-Lesson—Teacher Writing

The teacher presents a mini-lesson in which he models real writing and a skill or strategy. The mini-lesson has these elements:

- The mini-lesson focuses on writing, adding to, or editing a piece.
- The teacher refers to the Word Wall and other places in the room to model how words available in the room can help with spelling.
- The teacher models the use of an Editor's Checklist to promote and guide self-checking, peer revision, and editing. This checklist grows as appropriate expectations are added throughout the year.

15-20 min.

Segment Two: Children Writing and Conferencing

1. Students write on self-generated topics, individually paced at various stages of the writing process, perhaps working for multiple days on one piece.

2. Individual editing conferences occur between the day's designated students and the teacher while the other students write. Each student picks one piece, out of three to five good first drafts, to revise, edit, and publish during the conference.

5-10 min.

Segment Three: Sharing

1. Selected students share briefly in the Author's Chair (approximately two minutes each) something they have written.

2. The "author" answers several questions from classmates about the writing. The teacher models the types of thoughtful questions students should learn to ask each other.

TEACHER'S CHECKLIST FOR WRITING

In preparing and presenting my lesson in this block, I have...

_____ 1. Selected a skill or strategy to introduce in my mini-lesson that is necessary to improve my students' writing.

_____ 2. Provided a good model of writing, though not so sophisticated that students feel they cannot attain a similarly good piece of writing.

_____ 3. Modeled adding on to a piece of writing by occasionally beginning a piece one day and continuing to write it the next day.

_____ 4. Chosen a piece of my own writing occasionally to have students help me revise.

_____ 5. Modeled the use of resources in the classroom for spelling when writing, such as the Word Wall, charts, pictures, and theme boards.

_____ 6. Modeled how a student might "stretch-out" a word to figure out a temporary spelling.

_____ 7. Varied the topic, purpose, and audience of my mini-lessons on different days.

_____ 8. Encouraged students to write on their own topics.

_____ 9. Modeled during Author's Chair the types of higher-level questions about writing that students should ask of themselves and their peers.

_____ 10. Provided motivation for writing through several avenues of publishing, such as making a book, displaying work in the classroom or halls, or sharing via e-mail with another class.

_____ 11. Developed an Editor's Checklist to assist students with self- and peer-editing of their work.

_____ 12. Included some focused writing weeks to teach particular types of writing in Grades 2 and 3.

Please refer to pages 102-104 for additional information, ideas, and activities for the Writing Block.

Information appears in *The Teacher's Guide to the Four Blocks®* and *Implementing the 4-Blocks® Model*.

SUMMARY OF THE
WORKING WITH WORDS BLOCK

Purpose: To ensure that children read, spell, and use high-frequency words correctly, and that they learn the patterns necessary for decoding and spelling.

Total Time: 30 minutes (Pacing is critical!)

10 min.

Segment One: Word Wall

The teacher introduces five Word Wall words each week by having students do the following:

- See the words, then <u>say</u> the words.
- Chant the words (snap, clap, stomp, cheer, etc.).
- Write the words and check them together with the teacher.
- Trace around the words and check them together with the teacher.
- Do *On-the-Back* activities involving the words.

On days of the week when new Word Wall words are not the focus, the teacher reviews previous Word Wall words. When children can cheer for, write, and check five words in less than ten minutes, the remaining minutes are used for an *On-the-Back* activity.

20 min.

Segment Two: Decoding/Spelling Activity

The teacher guides activities to help children learn spelling patterns, which may include any of the following:

- **Making Words**—children manipulate letters of the alphabet to construct words, sort words into patterns, and use the sorted rhyming words to spell and read new words.
- **Guess the Covered Word**—students learn to cross check meaning and letter-sound relationships.
- **Using Words You Know**—children learn how the words they already know can help them read and spell lots of other words.
- **Rounding Up the Rhymes**—emphasizes spelling and rhyming patterns.
- **Reading/Writing Rhymes**—students use rhyming words to write and read silly rhymes.

TEACHER'S CHECKLIST FOR
WORKING WITH WORDS

In preparing and presenting my lesson in this block, I have...

_____ 1. Added only words to the Word Wall which are used frequently in reading and writing at this grade, and which should be spelled and used correctly.

_____ 2. Provided a good written and spoken model of the correct spelling and pronunciation of each of the Word Wall words.

_____ 3. Found ways (other than the Word Wall) to display words, other than high-frequency words, that students will want to use in their writing. I have meaningfully clustered the words (colors, numbers, theme charts) for easy access.

_____ 4. Practiced Word Wall words by chanting and writing. Included *On-the-Back* activities that help students explore words and transfer their learning to other words.

_____ 5. Planned *Making Words* activities which include small words, bigger words, and a secret word; sorted for patterns; and transferred sorted rhymes and patterns to read and spell a few new words.

_____ 6. Briskly paced my *Making Words* lesson by not waiting for each child to correctly spell the given word before sending a student to the chart to share the correct spelling with the class. Then, I have encouraged all students to check and spell correctly.

_____ 7. Planned *Guess the Covered Word* activities using all the onsets and led children to see that guessing a word that just makes sense is not particularly helpful, but guessing a word that makes sense, has all the correct beginning letters, and is about the right length is a very helpful decoding strategy.

_____ 8. Planned *Rounding Up the Rhymes*, *Using Words You Know*, and *Reading/Writing Rhymes* activities so that students learned a variety of rhyming patterns and used these to read and spell words.

_____ 9. Made sure that other activities included in the Working with Words Block helped children learn patterns, stressed transfer to reading and spelling new words, and were multilevel.

Please refer to pages 105-110 for additional information, ideas, and activities for the Working with Words Block.

Information appears in *The Teacher's Guide to the Four Blocks®* and *Implementing the 4-Blocks® Model*.

Week of _____

Monday	
Tuesday	
Wednesday	
Thursday	
Friday	

Special Events This Week:

FOUR-BLOCKS WEEKLY RECORD

❒ Guided Reading

Before (5-10 min.)
During (15-20 min.)
After (5-10 min.)

30-40 min.

M Before _____
  During _____
  After _____

T Before _____
  During _____
  After _____

W Before _____
  During _____
  After _____

Th Before _____
  During _____
  After _____

F Before _____
  During _____
  After _____

❒ Self-Selected Reading

Teacher Read-Aloud (5-10 min.)

30-40 min.

M _____
T _____
W _____
Th _____
F _____

Reading Conferences (15-20 min.)

M _____
  _____
T _____
  _____
W _____
  _____
Th _____
  _____
F _____
  _____

Sharing (5-10 min.)

M _____
T _____
W _____
Th _____
F _____

❒ Writing

Mini-Lesson (5-10 min.)

30-40 min.

M _____
T _____
W _____
Th _____
F _____

Writing/Conferences (15-20 min.)

M _____
  _____
T _____
  _____
W _____
  _____
Th _____
  _____
F _____
  _____

Sharing-Author's Chair (5-10 min.)

M _____
T _____
W _____
Th _____
F _____

❒ Working with Words

Word Wall Words (10 min.)

30 min.

_____ _____
_____ _____

On-The-Back Activity (see page 105)

M _____
T _____
W _____
Th _____
F _____

Words Activity (20 min.)
(Circle appropriate day)

M T W Th F   Making Words
M T W Th F   Guess the Covered Word
M T W Th F   Using Words You Know
M T W Th F   Rounding Up the Rhymes
M T W Th F   Reading/Writing Rhymes
M T W Th F   Other _____

Week of _____

Monday	
Tuesday	
Wednesday	
Thursday	
Friday	

Special Events This Week:

FOUR-BLOCKS WEEKLY RECORD

❑ Guided Reading

Before (5-10 min.)
During (15-20 min.)
After (5-10 min.)

30-40 min.

M Before _____
During _____
After _____

T Before _____
During _____
After _____

W Before _____
During _____
After _____

Th Before _____
During _____
After _____

F Before _____
During _____
After _____

❑ Self-Selected Reading

Teacher Read-Aloud (5-10 min.)

30-40 min.

M _____
T _____
W _____
Th _____
F _____

Reading Conferences (15-20 min.)

M _____

T _____

W _____

Th _____

F _____

Sharing (5-10 min.)

M _____
T _____
W _____
Th _____
F _____

❑ Writing

Mini-Lesson (5-10 min.)

30-40 min.

M _____
T _____
W _____
Th _____
F _____

Writing/Conferences (15-20 min.)

M _____

T _____

W _____

Th _____

F _____

Sharing-Author's Chair (5-10 min.)

M _____
T _____
W _____
Th _____
F _____

❑ Working with Words

Word Wall Words (10 min.)

30 min.

_____ _____
_____ _____

On-The-Back Activity (see page 105)

M _____
T _____
W _____
Th _____
F _____

Words Activity (20 min.)
(Circle appropriate day)

M T W Th F   Making Words
M T W Th F   Guess the Covered Word
M T W Th F   Using Words You Know
M T W Th F   Rounding Up the Rhymes
M T W Th F   Reading/Writing Rhymes
M T W Th F   Other _____

Week of _____

Monday	
Tuesday	
Wednesday	
Thursday	
Friday	

Special Events This Week:

FOUR-BLOCKS WEEKLY RECORD

❐ Guided Reading

Before (5-10 min.)
During (15-20 min.)
After (5-10 min.)

30-40 min.

M Before _____
  During _____
  After _____
T Before _____
  During _____
  After _____
W Before _____
  During _____
  After _____
Th Before _____
  During _____
  After _____
F Before _____
  During _____
  After _____

❐ Self-Selected Reading

Teacher Read-Aloud (5-10 min.)

30-40 min.

M _____
T _____
W _____
Th _____
F _____

Reading Conferences (15-20 min.)

M _____
  _____
T _____
  _____
W _____
  _____
Th _____
  _____
F _____
  _____

Sharing (5-10 min.)

M _____
T _____
W _____
Th _____
F _____

❐ Writing

Mini-Lesson (5-10 min.)

30-40 min.

M _____
T _____
W _____
Th _____
F _____

Writing/Conferences (15-20 min.)

M _____

T _____

W _____

Th _____

F _____

Sharing-Author's Chair (5-10 min.)

M _____
T _____
W _____
Th _____
F _____

❐ Working with Words

Word Wall Words (10 min.)

30 min.

_____ _____
_____ _____

On-The-Back Activity (See page 105)

M _____
T _____
W _____
Th _____
F _____

Words Activity (20 min.)
(Circle appropriate day)

M T W Th F   Making Words
M T W Th F   Guess the Covered Word
M T W Th F   Using Words You Know
M T W Th F   Rounding Up the Rhymes
M T W Th F   Reading/Writing Rhymes
M T W Th F   Other _____

Week of _____

Monday	
Tuesday	
Wednesday	
Thursday	
Friday	

Special Events This Week:

❏ Guided Reading

30-40 min.

Before (5-10 min.)
During (15-20 min.)
After (5-10 min.)

M Before _____
   During _____
   After _____
T Before _____
   During _____
   After _____
W Before _____
   During _____
   After _____
Th Before _____
   During _____
   After _____
F Before _____
   During _____
   After _____

❏ Self-Selected Reading

30-40 min.

Teacher Read-Aloud (5-10 min.)

M _____
T _____
W _____
Th _____
F _____

Reading Conferences (15-20 min.)

M _____
T _____
W _____
Th _____
F _____

Sharing (5-10 min.)

M _____
T _____
W _____
Th _____
F _____

❏ Writing

30-40 min.

Mini-Lesson (5-10 min.)

M _____
T _____
W _____
Th _____
F _____

Writing/Conferences (15-20 min.)

M _____
T _____
W _____
Th _____
F _____

Sharing-Author's Chair (5-10 min.)

M _____
T _____
W _____
Th _____
F _____

❏ Working with Words

30 min.

Word Wall Words (10 min.)

_____
_____ _____
_____

On-The-Back Activity (See page 105)

M _____
T _____
W _____
Th _____
F _____

Words Activity (20 min.)
(Circle appropriate day)

M T W Th F   Making Words
M T W Th F   Guess the Covered Word
M T W Th F   Using Words You Know
M T W Th F   Rounding Up the Rhymes
M T W Th F   Reading/Writing Rhymes
M T W Th F   Other _____

Week of _____

Monday	
Tuesday	
Wednesday	
Thursday	
Friday	

Special Events This Week:

FOUR-BLOCKS WEEKLY RECORD

❏ Guided Reading

Before (5-10 min.)
During (15-20 min.)
After (5-10 min.)

30-40 min.

M Before _____
During _____
After _____

T Before _____
During _____
After _____

W Before _____
During _____
After _____

Th Before _____
During _____
After _____

F Before _____
During _____
After _____

❏ Self-Selected Reading

Teacher Read-Aloud (5-10 min.)

30-40 min.

M _____
T _____
W _____
Th _____
F _____

Reading Conferences (15-20 min.)

M _____
_____
T _____
_____
W _____
_____
Th _____
_____
F _____
_____

Sharing (5-10 min.)

M _____
T _____
W _____
Th _____
F _____

❏ Writing

Mini-Lesson (5-10 min.)

30-40 min.

M _____
T _____
W _____
Th _____
F _____

Writing/Conferences (15-20 min.)

M _____
_____
T _____
_____
W _____
_____
Th _____
_____
F _____
_____

Sharing-Author's Chair (5-10 min.)

M _____
T _____
W _____
Th _____
F _____

❏ Working with Words

Word Wall Words (10 min.)

30 min.

_____ _____
_____ _____
_____

On-The-Back Activity (See page 105)

M _____
T _____
W _____
Th _____
F _____

Words Activity (20 min.)
(Circle appropriate day)

M T W Th F   Making Words
M T W Th F   Guess the Covered Word
M T W Th F   Using Words You Know
M T W Th F   Rounding Up the Rhymes
M T W Th F   Reading/Writing Rhymes
M T W Th F   Other _____

Week of _____

Monday	
Tuesday	
Wednesday	
Thursday	
Friday	

Special Events This Week:

❏ **Guided Reading**　　　🕐 30-40 min.

Before (5-10 min.)
During (15-20 min.)
After (5-10 min.)

M　Before _____
　　During _____
　　After _____
T　Before _____
　　During _____
　　After _____
W　Before _____
　　During _____
　　After _____
Th　Before _____
　　During _____
　　After _____
F　Before _____
　　During _____
　　After _____

❏ **Self-Selected Reading**　🕐 30-40 min.

Teacher Read-Aloud (5-10 min.)

M　_____
T　_____
W　_____
Th　_____
F　_____

Reading Conferences (15-20 min.)

M　_____
　　_____
T　_____
　　_____
W　_____
　　_____
Th　_____
　　_____
F　_____
　　_____

Sharing (5-10 min.)

M　_____
T　_____
W　_____
Th　_____
F　_____

❏ **Writing**　　　　🕐 30-40 min.

Mini-Lesson (5-10 min.)

M　_____
T　_____
W　_____
Th　_____
F　_____

Writing/Conferences (15-20 min.)

M　_____
　　_____
T　_____
　　_____
W　_____
　　_____
Th　_____
　　_____
F　_____
　　_____

Sharing-Author's Chair (5-10 min.)

M　_____
T　_____
W　_____
Th　_____
F　_____

❏ **Working with Words**　🕐 30 min.

Word Wall Words (10 min.)

_____　_____
_____　_____
_____

On-The-Back Activity (See page 105)

M　_____
T　_____
W　_____
Th　_____
F　_____

Words Activity (20 min.)
(Circle appropriate day)

M T W Th F　　Making Words
M T W Th F　　Guess the Covered Word
M T W Th F　　Using Words You Know
M T W Th F　　Rounding Up the Rhymes
M T W Th F　　Reading/Writing Rhymes
M T W Th F　　Other _____

Week of _____

Monday	
Tuesday	
Wednesday	
Thursday	
Friday	

Special Events This Week:

FOUR-BLOCKS WEEKLY RECORD

❐ Guided Reading ◕ 30-40 min.

Before (5-10 min.)
During (15-20 min.)
After (5-10 min.)

M Before _____
  During _____
  After _____

T Before _____
  During _____
  After _____

W Before _____
  During _____
  After _____

Th Before _____
  During _____
  After _____

F Before _____
  During _____
  After _____

❐ Self-Selected Reading ◕ 30-40 min.

Teacher Read-Aloud (5-10 min.)

M _____
T _____
W _____
Th _____
F _____

Reading Conferences (15-20 min.)

M _____
  _____
T _____
  _____
W _____
  _____
Th _____
  _____
F _____
  _____

Sharing (5-10 min.)

M _____
T _____
W _____
Th _____
F _____

❐ Writing ◕ 30-40 min.

Mini-Lesson (5-10 min.)

M _____
T _____
W _____
Th _____
F _____

Writing/Conferences (15-20 min.)

M _____

T _____

W _____

Th _____

F _____

Sharing-Author's Chair (5-10 min.)

M _____
T _____
W _____
Th _____
F _____

❐ Working with Words ◔ 30 min.

Word Wall Words (10 min.)

_____ _____

_____ _____

On-The-Back Activity (See page 105)

M _____
T _____
W _____
Th _____
F _____

Words Activity (20 min.)
(Circle appropriate day)

M T W Th F Making Words
M T W Th F Guess the Covered Word
M T W Th F Using Words You Know
M T W Th F Rounding Up the Rhymes
M T W Th F Reading/Writing Rhymes
M T W Th F Other _____

Week of _____

Monday						
Tuesday						
Wednesday						
Thursday						
Friday						

Special Events This Week:

FOUR-BLOCKS WEEKLY RECORD

❏ Guided Reading

Before (5-10 min.)
During (15-20 min.)
After (5-10 min.)

30-40 min.

M Before _____
    During _____
    After _____
T Before _____
    During _____
    After _____
W Before _____
    During _____
    After _____
Th Before _____
    During _____
    After _____
F Before _____
    During _____
    After _____

❏ Self-Selected Reading

Teacher Read-Aloud (5-10 min.)

30-40 min.

M _____
T _____
W _____
Th _____
F _____

Reading Conferences (15-20 min.)

M _____
  _____
T _____
  _____
W _____
  _____
Th _____
  _____
F _____
  _____

Sharing (5-10 min.)

M _____
T _____
W _____
Th _____
F _____

❏ Writing

Mini-Lesson (5-10 min.)

30-40 min.

M _____
T _____
W _____
Th _____
F _____

Writing/Conferences (15-20 min.)

M _____
T _____
W _____
Th _____
F _____

Sharing-Author's Chair (5-10 min.)

M _____
T _____
W _____
Th _____
F _____

❏ Working with Words

Word Wall Words (10 min.)

30 min.

_____ _____
_____ _____
_____

On-The-Back Activity (See page 105)

M _____
T _____
W _____
Th _____
F _____

Words Activity (20 min.)
(Circle appropriate day)

M T W Th F   Making Words
M T W Th F   Guess the Covered Word
M T W Th F   Using Words You Know
M T W Th F   Rounding Up the Rhymes
M T W Th F   Reading/Writing Rhymes
M T W Th F   Other _____

Week of _____

Monday	
Tuesday	
Wednesday	
Thursday	
Friday	

Special Events This Week:

FOUR-BLOCKS WEEKLY RECORD

❒ Guided Reading

30-40 min.

Before (5-10 min.)
During (15-20 min.)
After (5-10 min.)

M Before _____
  During _____
  After _____
T Before _____
  During _____
  After _____
W Before _____
  During _____
  After _____
Th Before _____
  During _____
  After _____
F Before _____
  During _____
  After _____

❒ Self-Selected Reading

30-40 min.

Teacher Read-Aloud (5-10 min.)

M _____
T _____
W _____
Th _____
F _____

Reading Conferences (15-20 min.)

M _____
  _____
T _____
  _____
W _____
  _____
Th _____
  _____
F _____
  _____

Sharing (5-10 min.)

M _____
T _____
W _____
Th _____
F _____

❒ Writing

30-40 min.

Mini-Lesson (5-10 min.)

M _____
T _____
W _____
Th _____
F _____

Writing/Conferences (15-20 min.)

M _____
T _____
W _____
Th _____
F _____

Sharing-Author's Chair (5-10 min.)

M _____
T _____
W _____
Th _____
F _____

❒ Working with Words

30 min.

Word Wall Words (10 min.)

_____ _____
_____ _____
_____

On-The-Back Activity (See page 105)

M _____
T _____
W _____
Th _____
F _____

Words Activity (20 min.)

(Circle appropriate day)

M T W Th F   Making Words
M T W Th F   Guess the Covered Word
M T W Th F   Using Words You Know
M T W Th F   Rounding Up the Rhymes
M T W Th F   Reading/Writing Rhymes
M T W Th F   Other _____

Week of _____

Monday	
Tuesday	
Wednesday	
Thursday	
Friday	

Special Events This Week:

FOUR-BLOCKS WEEKLY RECORD

❏ Guided Reading

Before (5-10 min.)
During (15-20 min.)
After (5-10 min.)

30-40 min.

M Before _____
During _____
After _____
T Before _____
During _____
After _____
W Before _____
During _____
After _____
Th Before _____
During _____
After _____
F Before _____
During _____
After _____

❏ Self-Selected Reading

Teacher Read-Aloud (5-10 min.)

30-40 min.

M _____
T _____
W _____
Th _____
F _____

Reading Conferences (15-20 min.)

M _____

T _____

W _____

Th _____

F _____

Sharing (5-10 min.)

M _____
T _____
W _____
Th _____
F _____

❏ Writing

Mini-Lesson (5-10 min.)

30-40 min.

M _____
T _____
W _____
Th _____
F _____

Writing/Conferences (15-20 min.)

M _____

T _____

W _____

Th _____

F _____

Sharing-Author's Chair (5-10 min.)

M _____
T _____
W _____
Th _____
F _____

❏ Working with Words

Word Wall Words (10 min.)

30 min.

_____ _____
_____ _____
_____

On-The-Back Activity (See page 105)

M _____
T _____
W _____
Th _____
F _____

Words Activity (20 min.)
(Circle appropriate day)

M T W Th F   Making Words
M T W Th F   Guess the Covered Word
M T W Th F   Using Words You Know
M T W Th F   Rounding Up the Rhymes
M T W Th F   Reading/Writing Rhymes
M T W Th F   Other _____

Week of _____

Monday	
Tuesday	
Wednesday	
Thursday	
Friday	

Special Events This Week:

FOUR-BLOCKS WEEKLY RECORD

❏ Guided Reading

Before (5-10 min.)
During (15-20 min.)
After (5-10 min.)

⏱ 30-40 min.

M Before _____
    During _____
    After _____
T Before _____
    During _____
    After _____
W Before _____
    During _____
    After _____
Th Before _____
    During _____
    After _____
F Before _____
    During _____
    After _____

❏ Self-Selected Reading

Teacher Read-Aloud (5-10 min.)

⏱ 30-40 min.

M _____
T _____
W _____
Th _____
F _____

Reading Conferences (15-20 min.)

M _____
T _____
W _____
Th _____
F _____

Sharing (5-10 min.)

M _____
T _____
W _____
Th _____
F _____

❏ Writing

Mini-Lesson (5-10 min.)

⏱ 30-40 min.

M _____
T _____
W _____
Th _____
F _____

Writing/Conferences (15-20 min.)

M _____
T _____
W _____
Th _____
F _____

Sharing-Author's Chair (5-10 min.)

M _____
T _____
W _____
Th _____
F _____

❏ Working with Words

Word Wall Words (10 min.)

⏱ 30 min.

_____   _____
_____   _____

On-The-Back Activity (See page 105)

M _____
T _____
W _____
Th _____
F _____

Words Activity (20 min.)
(Circle appropriate day)

M T W Th F   Making Words
M T W Th F   Guess the Covered Word
M T W Th F   Using Words You Know
M T W Th F   Rounding Up the Rhymes
M T W Th F   Reading/Writing Rhymes
M T W Th F   Other _____

Week of _____

Monday	
Tuesday	
Wednesday	
Thursday	
Friday	

Special Events This Week:

FOUR-BLOCKS WEEKLY RECORD

❏ Guided Reading
30-40 min.

Before (5-10 min.)
During (15-20 min.)
After (5-10 min.)

M Before _____
   During _____
   After _____
T Before _____
   During _____
   After _____
W Before _____
   During _____
   After _____
Th Before _____
   During _____
   After _____
F Before _____
   During _____
   After _____

❏ Self-Selected Reading
30-40 min.

Teacher Read-Aloud (5-10 min.)

M _____
T _____
W _____
Th _____
F _____

Reading Conferences (15-20 min.)

M _____
   _____
T _____
   _____
W _____
   _____
Th _____
   _____
F _____
   _____

Sharing (5-10 min.)

M _____
T _____
W _____
Th _____
F _____

❏ Writing
30-40 min.

Mini-Lesson (5-10 min.)

M _____
T _____
W _____
Th _____
F _____

Writing/Conferences (15-20 min.)

M _____
   _____
T _____
   _____
W _____
   _____
Th _____
   _____
F _____
   _____

Sharing-Author's Chair (5-10 min.)

M _____
T _____
W _____
Th _____
F _____

❏ Working with Words
30 min.

Word Wall Words (10 min.)

_____ _____
_____ _____
_____

On-The-Back Activity (See page 105)

M _____
T _____
W _____
Th _____
F _____

Words Activity (20 min.)
(Circle appropriate day)

M T W Th F Making Words
M T W Th F Guess the Covered Word
M T W Th F Using Words You Know
M T W Th F Rounding Up the Rhymes
M T W Th F Reading/Writing Rhymes
M T W Th F Other _____

Week of _____

Monday	
Tuesday	
Wednesday	
Thursday	
Friday	

Special Events This Week:

FOUR-BLOCKS WEEKLY RECORD

❐ Guided Reading

Before (5-10 min.)
During (15-20 min.)
After (5-10 min.)

30-40 min.

M Before _____
   During _____
   After _____

T Before _____
   During _____
   After _____

W Before _____
   During _____
   After _____

Th Before _____
   During _____
   After _____

F Before _____
   During _____
   After _____

❐ Self-Selected Reading

Teacher Read-Aloud (5-10 min.)

30-40 min.

M _____
T _____
W _____
Th _____
F _____

Reading Conferences (15-20 min.)

M _____

T _____

W _____

Th _____

F _____

Sharing (5-10 min.)

M _____
T _____
W _____
Th _____
F _____

❐ Writing

Mini-Lesson (5-10 min.)

30-40 min.

M _____
T _____
W _____
Th _____
F _____

Writing/Conferences (15-20 min.)

M _____

T _____

W _____

Th _____

F _____

Sharing-Author's Chair (5-10 min.)

M _____
T _____
W _____
Th _____
F _____

❐ Working with Words

Word Wall Words (10 min.)

30 min.

_____ _____

_____ _____

_____

On-The-Back Activity (See page 105)

M _____
T _____
W _____
Th _____
F _____

Words Activity (20 min.)
(Circle appropriate day)

M T W Th F   Making Words
M T W Th F   Guess the Covered Word
M T W Th F   Using Words You Know
M T W Th F   Rounding Up the Rhymes
M T W Th F   Reading/Writing Rhymes
M T W Th F   Other _____

Week of _____

Monday	
Tuesday	
Wednesday	
Thursday	
Friday	

Special Events This Week:

FOUR-BLOCKS WEEKLY RECORD

❏ Guided Reading   ⏰ 30-40 min.

Before (5-10 min.)
During (15-20 min.)
After (5-10 min.)

M   Before _____
     During _____
     After _____

T   Before _____
     During _____
     After _____

W   Before _____
     During _____
     After _____

Th   Before _____
     During _____
     After _____

F   Before _____
     During _____
     After _____

❏ Self-Selected Reading   ⏰ 30-40 min.

Teacher Read-Aloud (5-10 min.)

M _____
T _____
W _____
Th _____
F _____

Reading Conferences (15-20 min.)

M _____
   _____
T _____
   _____
W _____
   _____
Th _____
   _____
F _____
   _____

Sharing (5-10 min.)

M _____
T _____
W _____
Th _____
F _____

❏ Writing   ⏰ 30-40 min.

Mini-Lesson (5-10 min.)

M _____
T _____
W _____
Th _____
F _____

Writing/Conferences (15-20 min.)

M _____
   _____
T _____
   _____
W _____
   _____
Th _____
   _____
F _____
   _____

Sharing-Author's Chair (5-10 min.)

M _____
T _____
W _____
Th _____
F _____

❏ Working with Words   ⏰ 30 min.

Word Wall Words (10 min.)

_____   _____
_____   _____

On-The-Back Activity (See page 105)

M _____
T _____
W _____
Th _____
F _____

Words Activity (20 min.)
(Circle appropriate day)

M T W Th F   Making Words
M T W Th F   Guess the Covered Word
M T W Th F   Using Words You Know
M T W Th F   Rounding Up the Rhymes
M T W Th F   Reading/Writing Rhymes
M T W Th F   Other _____

Week of _____

Monday	
Tuesday	
Wednesday	
Thursday	
Friday	

Special Events This Week:

FOUR-BLOCKS WEEKLY RECORD

❏ Guided Reading

Before (5-10 min.)
During (15-20 min.)
After (5-10 min.)

30-40 min.

M Before _____
    During _____
    After _____
T Before _____
    During _____
    After _____
W Before _____
    During _____
    After _____
Th Before _____
    During _____
    After _____
F Before _____
    During _____
    After _____

❏ Self-Selected Reading

Teacher Read-Aloud (5-10 min.)

30-40 min.

M _____
T _____
W _____
Th _____
F _____

Reading Conferences (15-20 min.)

M _____
    _____
T _____
    _____
W _____
    _____
Th _____
    _____
F _____
    _____

Sharing (5-10 min.)

M _____
T _____
W _____
Th _____
F _____

❏ Writing

Mini-Lesson (5-10 min.)

30-40 min.

M _____
T _____
W _____
Th _____
F _____

Writing/Conferences (15-20 min.)

M _____
    _____
T _____
    _____
W _____
    _____
Th _____
    _____
F _____
    _____

Sharing-Author's Chair (5-10 min.)

M _____
T _____
W _____
Th _____
F _____

❏ Working with Words

Word Wall Words (10 min.)

30 min.

_____   _____
_____   _____
_____

On-The-Back Activity (See page 105)

M _____
T _____
W _____
Th _____
F _____

Words Activity (20 min.)
(Circle appropriate day)

M T W Th F   Making Words
M T W Th F   Guess the Covered Word
M T W Th F   Using Words You Know
M T W Th F   Rounding Up the Rhymes
M T W Th F   Reading/Writing Rhymes
M T W Th F   Other _____

Week of _____

Monday	
Tuesday	
Wednesday	
Thursday	
Friday	

Special Events This Week:

FOUR-BLOCKS WEEKLY RECORD

❏ Guided Reading

Before (5-10 min.)
During (15-20 min.)
After (5-10 min.)

30-40 min.

M Before _____
  During _____
  After _____
T Before _____
  During _____
  After _____
W Before _____
  During _____
  After _____
Th Before _____
  During _____
  After _____
F Before _____
  During _____
  After _____

❏ Self-Selected Reading

Teacher Read-Aloud (5-10 min.)

30-40 min.

M _____
T _____
W _____
Th _____
F _____

Reading Conferences (15-20 min.)

M _____
T _____
W _____
Th _____
F _____

Sharing (5-10 min.)

M _____
T _____
W _____
Th _____
F _____

❏ Writing

Mini-Lesson (5-10 min.)

30-40 min.

M _____
T _____
W _____
Th _____
F _____

Writing/Conferences (15-20 min.)

M _____
_____
T _____
_____
W _____
_____
Th _____
_____
F _____
_____

Sharing-Author's Chair (5-10 min.)

M _____
T _____
W _____
Th _____
F _____

❏ Working with Words

Word Wall Words (10 min.)

30 min.

_____ _____
_____ _____
_____

On-The-Back Activity (See page 105)

M _____
T _____
W _____
Th _____
F _____

Words Activity (20 min.)
(Circle appropriate day)

M T W Th F   Making Words
M T W Th F   Guess the Covered Word
M T W Th F   Using Words You Know
M T W Th F   Rounding Up the Rhymes
M T W Th F   Reading/Writing Rhymes
M T W Th F   Other _____

Week of _____

Monday	
Tuesday	
Wednesday	
Thursday	
Friday	

Special Events This Week:

FOUR-BLOCKS WEEKLY RECORD

❏ Guided Reading

Before (5-10 min.)
During (15-20 min.)
After (5-10 min.)

30-40 min.

M Before _____
During _____
After _____

T Before _____
During _____
After _____

W Before _____
During _____
After _____

Th Before _____
During _____
After _____

F Before _____
During _____
After _____

❏ Self-Selected Reading

Teacher Read-Aloud (5-10 min.)

30-40 min.

M _____
T _____
W _____
Th _____
F _____

Reading Conferences (15-20 min.)

M _____
_____

T _____
_____

W _____
_____

Th _____
_____

F _____
_____

Sharing (5-10 min.)

M _____
T _____
W _____
Th _____
F _____

❏ Writing

Mini-Lesson (5-10 min.)

30-40 min.

M _____
T _____
W _____
Th _____
F _____

Writing/Conferences (15-20 min.)

M _____
_____

T _____
_____

W _____
_____

Th _____
_____

F _____
_____

Sharing-Author's Chair (5-10 min.)

M _____
T _____
W _____
Th _____
F _____

❏ Working with Words

Word Wall Words (10 min.)

30 min.

_____ _____
_____ _____
_____

On-The-Back Activity (See page 105)

M _____
T _____
W _____
Th _____
F _____

Words Activity (20 min.)
(Circle appropriate day)

M T W Th F   Making Words
M T W Th F   Guess the Covered Word
M T W Th F   Using Words You Know
M T W Th F   Rounding Up the Rhymes
M T W Th F   Reading/Writing Rhymes
M T W Th F   Other _____

Week of _____

Monday	
Tuesday	
Wednesday	
Thursday	
Friday	

Special Events This Week:

FOUR-BLOCKS WEEKLY RECORD

❐ Guided Reading

Before (5-10 min.)
During (15-20 min.)
After (5-10 min.)

30-40 min.

M Before _____
   During _____
   After _____
T Before _____
   During _____
   After _____
W Before _____
   During _____
   After _____
Th Before _____
   During _____
   After _____
F Before _____
   During _____
   After _____

❐ Self-Selected Reading

Teacher Read-Aloud (5-10 min.)

30-40 min.

M _____
T _____
W _____
Th _____
F _____

Reading Conferences (15-20 min.)

M _____
T _____
W _____
Th _____
F _____

Sharing (5-10 min.)

M _____
T _____
W _____
Th _____
F _____

❐ Writing

Mini-Lesson (5-10 min.)

30-40 min.

M _____
T _____
W _____
Th _____
F _____

Writing/Conferences (15-20 min.)

M _____
T _____
W _____
Th _____
F _____

Sharing-Author's Chair (5-10 min.)

M _____
T _____
W _____
Th _____
F _____

❐ Working with Words

Word Wall Words (10 min.)

30 min.

_____   _____
_____   _____

On-The-Back Activity (See page 105)

M _____
T _____
W _____
Th _____
F _____

Words Activity (20 min.)
(Circle appropriate day)

M T W Th F   Making Words
M T W Th F   Guess the Covered Word
M T W Th F   Using Words You Know
M T W Th F   Rounding Up the Rhymes
M T W Th F   Reading/Writing Rhymes
M T W Th F   Other _____

Week of _____

Monday	
Tuesday	
Wednesday	
Thursday	
Friday	

Special Events This Week:

FOUR-BLOCKS WEEKLY RECORD

❐ Guided Reading
Before (5-10 min.)
During (15-20 min.)
After (5-10 min.)

M Before _____
    During _____
    After _____
T   Before _____
    During _____
    After _____
W   Before _____
    During _____
    After _____
Th Before _____
    During _____
    After _____
F   Before _____
    During _____
    After _____

❐ Self-Selected Reading
Teacher Read-Aloud (5-10 min.)

M _____
T _____
W _____
Th _____
F _____

Reading Conferences (15-20 min.)

M _____

T _____

W _____

Th _____

_____

F _____

_____

Sharing (5-10 min.)

M _____
T _____
W _____
Th _____
F _____

❐ Writing
Mini-Lesson (5-10 min.)

M _____
T _____
W _____
Th _____
F _____

Writing/Conferences (15-20 min.)

M _____

T _____

W _____

Th _____

F _____

Sharing-Author's Chair (5-10 min.)

M _____
T _____
W _____
Th _____
F _____

❐ Working with Words
Word Wall Words (10 min.)

_____ _____

_____ _____

On-The-Back Activity (See page 105)

M _____
T _____
W _____
Th _____
F _____

Words Activity (20 min.)
(Circle appropriate day)

M T W Th F Making Words
M T W Th F Guess the Covered Word
M T W Th F Using Words You Know
M T W Th F Rounding Up the Rhymes
M T W Th F Reading/Writing Rhymes
M T W Th F Other _____

Week of _____

Monday	
Tuesday	
Wednesday	
Thursday	
Friday	

Special Events This Week:

FOUR-BLOCKS WEEKLY RECORD

❑ Guided Reading

Before (5-10 min.)
During (15-20 min.)
After (5-10 min.)

30-40 min.

M Before _____
    During _____
    After _____

T Before _____
    During _____
    After _____

W Before _____
    During _____
    After _____

Th Before _____
    During _____
    After _____

F Before _____
    During _____
    After _____

❑ Self-Selected Reading

Teacher Read-Aloud (5-10 min.)

30-40 min.

M _____
T _____
W _____
Th _____
F _____

Reading Conferences (15-20 min.)

M _____

T _____

W _____

Th _____

F _____

Sharing (5-10 min.)

M _____
T _____
W _____
Th _____
F _____

❑ Writing

Mini-Lesson (5-10 min.)

30-40 min.

M _____
T _____
W _____
Th _____
F _____

Writing/Conferences (15-20 min.)

M _____

T _____

W _____

Th _____

F _____

Sharing-Author's Chair (5-10 min.)

M _____
T _____
W _____
Th _____
F _____

❑ Working with Words

Word Wall Words (10 min.)

30 min.

_____ _____

_____ _____

On-The-Back Activity (See page 105)

M _____
T _____
W _____
Th _____
F _____

Words Activity (20 min.)
(Circle appropriate day)

M T W Th F Making Words
M T W Th F Guess the Covered Word
M T W Th F Using Words You Know
M T W Th F Rounding Up the Rhymes
M T W Th F Reading/Writing Rhymes
M T W Th F Other _____

Week of _____

Monday	
Tuesday	
Wednesday	
Thursday	
Friday	

Special Events This Week:

FOUR-BLOCKS WEEKLY RECORD

❏ Guided Reading

Before (5-10 min.)
During (15-20 min.)
After (5-10 min.)

30-40 min.

M Before _____
   During _____
   After _____
T Before _____
   During _____
   After _____
W Before _____
   During _____
   After _____
Th Before _____
   During _____
   After _____
F Before _____
   During _____
   After _____

❏ Self-Selected Reading

Teacher Read-Aloud (5-10 min.)

30-40 min.

M _____
T _____
W _____
Th _____
F _____

Reading Conferences (15-20 min.)

M _____
  _____
T _____
  _____
W _____
  _____
Th _____
  _____
F _____
  _____

Sharing (5-10 min.)

M _____
T _____
W _____
Th _____
F _____

❏ Writing

Mini-Lesson (5-10 min.)

30-40 min.

M _____
T _____
W _____
Th _____
F _____

Writing/Conferences (15-20 min.)

M _____
  _____
T _____
  _____
W _____
  _____
Th _____
  _____
F _____
  _____

Sharing-Author's Chair (5-10 min.)

M _____
T _____
W _____
Th _____
F _____

❏ Working with Words

Word Wall Words (10 min.)

30 min.

_____ _____
_____ _____
_____

On-The-Back Activity (See page 105)

M _____
T _____
W _____
Th _____
F _____

Words Activity (20 min.)
(Circle appropriate day)

M T W Th F   Making Words
M T W Th F   Guess the Covered Word
M T W Th F   Using Words You Know
M T W Th F   Rounding Up the Rhymes
M T W Th F   Reading/Writing Rhymes
M T W Th F   Other _____

Week of _____

Monday	
Tuesday	
Wednesday	
Thursday	
Friday	

Special Events This Week:

FOUR-BLOCKS WEEKLY RECORD

❒ Guided Reading

Before (5-10 min.)
During (15-20 min.)
After (5-10 min.)

30-40 min.

M Before _____
  During _____
  After _____
T Before _____
  During _____
  After _____
W Before _____
  During _____
  After _____
Th Before _____
   During _____
   After _____
F Before _____
  During _____
  After _____

❒ Self-Selected Reading

Teacher Read-Aloud (5-10 min.)

30-40 min.

M _____
T _____
W _____
Th _____
F _____

Reading Conferences (15-20 min.)

M _____
  _____
T _____
  _____
W _____
  _____
Th _____
   _____
F _____
  _____

Sharing (5-10 min.)

M _____
T _____
W _____
Th _____
F _____

❒ Writing

Mini-Lesson (5-10 min.)

30-40 min.

M _____
T _____
W _____
Th _____
F _____

Writing/Conferences (15-20 min.)

M _____

T _____

W _____

Th _____

F _____

Sharing-Author's Chair (5-10 min.)

M _____
T _____
W _____
Th _____
F _____

❒ Working with Words

Word Wall Words (10 min.)

30 min.

_____ _____
_____ _____
_____

On-The-Back Activity (See page 105)

M _____
T _____
W _____
Th _____
F _____

Words Activity (20 min.)
(Circle appropriate day)

M T W Th F   Making Words
M T W Th F   Guess the Covered Word
M T W Th F   Using Words You Know
M T W Th F   Rounding Up the Rhymes
M T W Th F   Reading/Writing Rhymes
M T W Th F   Other _____

Week of _____

Monday	
Tuesday	
Wednesday	
Thursday	
Friday	

Special Events This Week:

❏ **Guided Reading** 30-40 min.
Before (5-10 min.)
During (15-20 min.)
After (5-10 min.)

M Before _____
During _____
After _____
T Before _____
During _____
After _____
W Before _____
During _____
After _____
Th Before _____
During _____
After _____
F Before _____
During _____
After _____

❏ **Self-Selected Reading** 30-40 min.
Teacher Read-Aloud (5-10 min.)
M _____
T _____
W _____
Th _____
F _____

Reading Conferences (15-20 min.)
M _____
_____
T _____
_____
W _____
_____
Th _____
_____
F _____
_____

Sharing (5-10 min.)
M _____
T _____
W _____
Th _____
F _____

❏ **Writing** 30-40 min.
Mini-Lesson (5-10 min.)
M _____
T _____
W _____
Th _____
F _____

Writing/Conferences (15-20 min.)
M _____
_____
T _____
_____
W _____
_____
Th _____
_____
F _____
_____

Sharing-Author's Chair (5-10 min.)
M _____
T _____
W _____
Th _____
F _____

❏ **Working with Words** 30 min.
Word Wall Words (10 min.)
_____
_____ _____
_____

On-The-Back Activity (See page 105)
M _____
T _____
W _____
Th _____
F _____

Words Activity (20 min.)
(Circle appropriate day)
M T W Th F   Making Words
M T W Th F   Guess the Covered Word
M T W Th F   Using Words You Know
M T W Th F   Rounding Up the Rhymes
M T W Th F   Reading/Writing Rhymes
M T W Th F   Other _____

Week of _____

Monday	
Tuesday	
Wednesday	
Thursday	
Friday	

Special Events This Week:

FOUR-BLOCKS WEEKLY RECORD

❏ **Guided Reading** 30-40 min.

Before (5-10 min.)
During (15-20 min.)
After (5-10 min.)

M Before _____
  During _____
  After _____
T Before _____
  During _____
  After _____
W Before _____
  During _____
  After _____
Th Before _____
  During _____
  After _____
F Before _____
  During _____
  After _____

❏ **Self-Selected Reading** 30-40 min.

Teacher Read-Aloud (5-10 min.)

M _____
T _____
W _____
Th _____
F _____

Reading Conferences (15-20 min.)

M _____
  _____
T _____
  _____
W _____
  _____
Th _____
  _____
F _____
  _____

Sharing (5-10 min.)

M _____
T _____
W _____
Th _____
F _____

❏ **Writing** 30-40 min.

Mini-Lesson (5-10 min.)

M _____
T _____
W _____
Th _____
F _____

Writing/Conferences (15-20 min.)

M _____
T _____
W _____
Th _____
F _____

Sharing-Author's Chair (5-10 min.)

M _____
T _____
W _____
Th _____
F _____

❏ **Working with Words** 30 min.

Word Wall Words (10 min.)

_____ _____
_____ _____
_____

On-The-Back Activity (See page 105)

M _____
T _____
W _____
Th _____
F _____

Words Activity (20 min.)
(Circle appropriate day)

M T W Th F   Making Words
M T W Th F   Guess the Covered Word
M T W Th F   Using Words You Know
M T W Th F   Rounding Up the Rhymes
M T W Th F   Reading/Writing Rhymes
M T W Th F   Other _____

Week of _____

Monday	
Tuesday	
Wednesday	
Thursday	
Friday	

Special Events This Week:

FOUR-BLOCKS WEEKLY RECORD

❏ Guided Reading

Before (5-10 min.)
During (15-20 min.)
After (5-10 min.)

M Before _____
   During _____
   After _____
T Before _____
   During _____
   After _____
W Before _____
   During _____
   After _____
Th Before _____
   During _____
   After _____
F Before _____
   During _____
   After _____

❏ Self-Selected Reading

Teacher Read-Aloud (5-10 min.)

M _____
T _____
W _____
Th _____
F _____

Reading Conferences (15-20 min.)

M _____
   _____
T _____
   _____
W _____
   _____
Th _____
   _____
F _____
   _____

Sharing (5-10 min.)

M _____
T _____
W _____
Th _____
F _____

❏ Writing

Mini-Lesson (5-10 min.)

M _____
T _____
W _____
Th _____
F _____

Writing/Conferences (15-20 min.)

M _____
T _____
W _____
Th _____
F _____

Sharing-Author's Chair (5-10 min.)

M _____
T _____
W _____
Th _____
F _____

❏ Working with Words

Word Wall Words (10 min.)

_____   _____
_____   _____
_____

On-The-Back Activity (See page 105)

M _____
T _____
W _____
Th _____
F _____

Words Activity (20 min.)
(Circle appropriate day)

M T W Th F   Making Words
M T W Th F   Guess the Covered Word
M T W Th F   Using Words You Know
M T W Th F   Rounding Up the Rhymes
M T W Th F   Reading/Writing Rhymes
M T W Th F   Other _____

Week of _____

Monday	
Tuesday	
Wednesday	
Thursday	
Friday	

Special Events This Week:

FOUR-BLOCKS WEEKLY RECORD

❐ Guided Reading

30-40 min.

Before (5-10 min.)
During (15-20 min.)
After (5-10 min.)

M Before _____
   During _____
   After _____

T Before _____
   During _____
   After _____

W Before _____
   During _____
   After _____

Th Before _____
   During _____
   After _____

F Before _____
   During _____
   After _____

❐ Self-Selected Reading

30-40 min.

Teacher Read-Aloud (5-10 min.)

M _____
T _____
W _____
Th _____
F _____

Reading Conferences (15-20 min.)

M _____
  _____
T _____
  _____
W _____
  _____
Th _____
  _____
F _____
  _____

Sharing (5-10 min.)

M _____
T _____
W _____
Th _____
F _____

❐ Writing

30-40 min.

Mini-Lesson (5-10 min.)

M _____
T _____
W _____
Th _____
F _____

Writing/Conferences (15-20 min.)

M _____
T _____
W _____
Th _____
F _____

Sharing-Author's Chair (5-10 min.)

M _____
T _____
W _____
Th _____
F _____

❐ Working with Words

30 min.

Word Wall Words (10 min.)

_____ _____
_____ _____
_____

On-The-Back Activity (See page 105)

M _____
T _____
W _____
Th _____
F _____

Words Activity (20 min.)
(Circle appropriate day)

M T W Th F   Making Words
M T W Th F   Guess the Covered Word
M T W Th F   Using Words You Know
M T W Th F   Rounding Up the Rhymes
M T W Th F   Reading/Writing Rhymes
M T W Th F   Other _____

Week of _____

Monday	
Tuesday	
Wednesday	
Thursday	
Friday	

Special Events This Week:

FOUR-BLOCKS WEEKLY RECORD

❒ **Guided Reading**　　　30-40 min.

Before (5-10 min.)
During (15-20 min.)
After (5-10 min.)

M　Before _____
　　During _____
　　After _____
T　Before _____
　　During _____
　　After _____
W　Before _____
　　During _____
　　After _____
Th Before _____
　　During _____
　　After _____
F　Before _____
　　During _____
　　After _____

❒ **Self-Selected Reading**　　30-40 min.

Teacher Read-Aloud (5-10 min.)

M _____
T _____
W _____
Th _____
F _____

Reading Conferences (15-20 min.)

M _____
　 _____
T _____
　 _____
W _____
　 _____
Th _____
　 _____
F _____
　 _____

Sharing (5-10 min.)

M _____
T _____
W _____
Th _____
F _____

❒ **Writing**　　　30-40 min.

Mini-Lesson (5-10 min.)

M _____
T _____
W _____
Th _____
F _____

Writing/Conferences (15-20 min.)

M _____
　 _____
T _____
　 _____
W _____
　 _____
Th _____
　 _____
F _____
　 _____

Sharing-Author's Chair (5-10 min.)

M _____
T _____
W _____
Th _____
F _____

❒ **Working with Words**　　30 min.

Word Wall Words (10 min.)

_____ _____
_____ _____
_____

On-The-Back Activity (See page 105)

M _____
T _____
W _____
Th _____
F _____

Words Activity (20 min.)

(Circle appropriate day)

M T W Th F　Making Words
M T W Th F　Guess the Covered Word
M T W Th F　Using Words You Know
M T W Th F　Rounding Up the Rhymes
M T W Th F　Reading/Writing Rhymes
M T W Th F　Other _____

Week of _____

Monday	
Tuesday	
Wednesday	
Thursday	
Friday	

Special Events This Week:

FOUR-BLOCKS WEEKLY RECORD

❑ Guided Reading

Before (5-10 min.)
During (15-20 min.)
After (5-10 min.)

30-40 min.

M Before _____
   During _____
   After _____

T Before _____
   During _____
   After _____

W Before _____
   During _____
   After _____

Th Before _____
   During _____
   After _____

F Before _____
   During _____
   After _____

❑ Self-Selected Reading

Teacher Read-Aloud (5-10 min.) *30-40 min.*

M _____
T _____
W _____
Th _____
F _____

Reading Conferences (15-20 min.)

M _____
T _____
W _____
Th _____
F _____

Sharing (5-10 min.)

M _____
T _____
W _____
Th _____
F _____

❑ Writing

Mini-Lesson (5-10 min.) *30-40 min.*

M _____
T _____
W _____
Th _____
F _____

Writing/Conferences (15-20 min.)

M _____
T _____
W _____
Th _____
F _____

Sharing-Author's Chair (5-10 min.)

M _____
T _____
W _____
Th _____
F _____

❑ Working with Words

Word Wall Words (10 min.) *30 min.*

_____ _____
_____ _____

On-The-Back Activity (See page 105)

M _____
T _____
W _____
Th _____
F _____

Words Activity (20 min.)
(Circle appropriate day)

M T W Th F	Making Words
M T W Th F	Guess the Covered Word
M T W Th F	Using Words You Know
M T W Th F	Rounding Up the Rhymes
M T W Th F	Reading/Writing Rhymes
M T W Th F	Other _____

Week of _____

Monday	
Tuesday	
Wednesday	
Thursday	
Friday	

Special Events This Week:

FOUR-BLOCKS WEEKLY RECORD

❏ Guided Reading   30-40 min.

Before (5-10 min.)
During (15-20 min.)
After (5-10 min.)

M Before _____
    During _____
    After _____
T Before _____
    During _____
    After _____
W Before _____
    During _____
    After _____
Th Before _____
    During _____
    After _____
F Before _____
    During _____
    After _____

❏ Self-Selected Reading   30-40 min.

Teacher Read-Aloud (5-10 min.)

M _____
T _____
W _____
Th _____
F _____

Reading Conferences (15-20 min.)

M _____
    _____
T _____
    _____
W _____
    _____
Th _____
    _____
F _____
    _____

Sharing (5-10 min.)

M _____
T _____
W _____
Th _____
F _____

❏ Writing   30-40 min.

Mini-Lesson (5-10 min.)

M _____
T _____
W _____
Th _____
F _____

Writing/Conferences (15-20 min.)

M _____
T _____
W _____
Th _____
F _____

Sharing-Author's Chair (5-10 min.)

M _____
T _____
W _____
Th _____
F _____

❏ Working with Words   30 min.

Word Wall Words (10 min.)

_____ _____
_____ _____

On-The-Back Activity (See page 105)

M _____
T _____
W _____
Th _____
F _____

Words Activity (20 min.)
(Circle appropriate day)

M T W Th F Making Words
M T W Th F Guess the Covered Word
M T W Th F Using Words You Know
M T W Th F Rounding Up the Rhymes
M T W Th F Reading/Writing Rhymes
M T W Th F Other _____

Week of _____

Monday	
Tuesday	
Wednesday	
Thursday	
Friday	

Special Events This Week:

FOUR-BLOCKS WEEKLY RECORD

❏ Guided Reading

Before (5-10 min.)
During (15-20 min.)
After (5-10 min.)

30-40 min.

M Before _____
    During _____
    After _____

T Before _____
    During _____
    After _____

W Before _____
    During _____
    After _____

Th Before _____
    During _____
    After _____

F Before _____
    During _____
    After _____

❏ Self-Selected Reading

Teacher Read-Aloud (5-10 min.)

30-40 min.

M _____
T _____
W _____
Th _____
F _____

Reading Conferences (15-20 min.)

M _____
  _____
T _____
  _____
W _____
  _____
Th _____
  _____
F _____
  _____

Sharing (5-10 min.)

M _____
T _____
W _____
Th _____
F _____

❏ Writing

Mini-Lesson (5-10 min.)

30-40 min.

M _____
T _____
W _____
Th _____
F _____

Writing/Conferences (15-20 min.)

M _____
  _____
T _____
  _____
W _____
  _____
Th _____
  _____
F _____
  _____

Sharing-Author's Chair (5-10 min.)

M _____
T _____
W _____
Th _____
F _____

❏ Working with Words

Word Wall Words (10 min.)

30 min.

_____   _____
_____   _____

On-The-Back Activity (See page 105)

M _____
T _____
W _____
Th _____
F _____

Words Activity (20 min.)
(Circle appropriate day)

M T W Th F   Making Words
M T W Th F   Guess the Covered Word
M T W Th F   Using Words You Know
M T W Th F   Rounding Up the Rhymes
M T W Th F   Reading/Writing Rhymes
M T W Th F   Other _____

Week of _____

Monday	
Tuesday	
Wednesday	
Thursday	
Friday	

Special Events This Week:

FOUR-BLOCKS WEEKLY RECORD

❐ Guided Reading

Before (5-10 min.)
During (15-20 min.)
After (5-10 min.)

30-40 min.

M Before _____
   During _____
   After _____
T Before _____
   During _____
   After _____
W Before _____
   During _____
   After _____
Th Before _____
   During _____
   After _____
F Before _____
   During _____
   After _____

❐ Self-Selected Reading

Teacher Read-Aloud (5-10 min.)

30-40 min.

M _____
T _____
W _____
Th _____
F _____

Reading Conferences (15-20 min.)

M _____
   _____
T _____
   _____
W _____
   _____
Th _____
   _____
F _____
   _____

Sharing (5-10 min.)

M _____
T _____
W _____
Th _____
F _____

❐ Writing

Mini-Lesson (5-10 min.)

30-40 min.

M _____
T _____
W _____
Th _____
F _____

Writing/Conferences (15-20 min.)

M _____
T _____
W _____
Th _____
F _____

Sharing-Author's Chair (5-10 min.)

M _____
T _____
W _____
Th _____
F _____

❐ Working with Words

Word Wall Words (10 min.)

30 min.

_____ _____
_____ _____

On-The-Back Activity (See page 105)

M _____
T _____
W _____
Th _____
F _____

Words Activity (20 min.)
(Circle appropriate day)

M T W Th F   Making Words
M T W Th F   Guess the Covered Word
M T W Th F   Using Words You Know
M T W Th F   Rounding Up the Rhymes
M T W Th F   Reading/Writing Rhymes
M T W Th F   Other _____

Week of _____

Monday	
Tuesday	
Wednesday	
Thursday	
Friday	

Special Events This Week:

FOUR-BLOCKS WEEKLY RECORD

❏ Guided Reading

30-40 min.

Before (5-10 min.)
During (15-20 min.)
After (5-10 min.)

M Before _____
   During _____
   After _____
T Before _____
   During _____
   After _____
W Before _____
   During _____
   After _____
Th Before _____
   During _____
   After _____
F Before _____
   During _____
   After _____

❏ Self-Selected Reading

30-40 min.

Teacher Read-Aloud (5-10 min.)

M _____
T _____
W _____
Th _____
F _____

Reading Conferences (15-20 min.)

M _____
T _____
W _____
Th _____
F _____

Sharing (5-10 min.)

M _____
T _____
W _____
Th _____
F _____

❏ Writing

30-40 min.

Mini-Lesson (5-10 min.)

M _____
T _____
W _____
Th _____
F _____

Writing/Conferences (15-20 min.)

M _____
T _____
W _____
Th _____
F _____

Sharing-Author's Chair (5-10 min.)

M _____
T _____
W _____
Th _____
F _____

❏ Working with Words

30 min.

Word Wall Words (10 min.)

_____ _____
_____ _____

On-The-Back Activity (See page 105)

M _____
T _____
W _____
Th _____
F _____

Words Activity (20 min.)
(Circle appropriate day)

M T W Th F   Making Words
M T W Th F   Guess the Covered Word
M T W Th F   Using Words You Know
M T W Th F   Rounding Up the Rhymes
M T W Th F   Reading/Writing Rhymes
M T W Th F   Other _____

Week of _____

Monday	
Tuesday	
Wednesday	
Thursday	
Friday	

Special Events This Week:

FOUR-BLOCKS WEEKLY RECORD

❑ Guided Reading
Before (5-10 min.)
During (15-20 min.)
After (5-10 min.)

M	Before	_____
	During	_____
	After	_____
T	Before	_____
	During	_____
	After	_____
W	Before	_____
	During	_____
	After	_____
Th	Before	_____
	During	_____
	After	_____
F	Before	_____
	During	_____
	After	_____

30-40 min.

❑ Self-Selected Reading
Teacher Read-Aloud (5-10 min.)

M _____
T _____
W _____
Th _____
F _____

Reading Conferences (15-20 min.)

M _____
_____
T _____
_____
W _____
_____
Th _____
_____
F _____
_____

Sharing (5-10 min.)

M _____
T _____
W _____
Th _____
F _____

30-40 min.

❑ Writing
Mini-Lesson (5-10 min.)

M _____
T _____
W _____
Th _____
F _____

Writing/Conferences (15-20 min.)

M _____
_____
T _____
_____
W _____
_____
Th _____
_____
F _____
_____

Sharing-Author's Chair (5-10 min.)

M _____
T _____
W _____
Th _____
F _____

30-40 min.

❑ Working with Words
Word Wall Words (10 min.)

_____ _____
_____ _____
_____

On-The-Back Activity (See page 105)

M _____
T _____
W _____
Th _____
F _____

Words Activity (20 min.)
(Circle appropriate day)

M T W Th F	Making Words
M T W Th F	Guess the Covered Word
M T W Th F	Using Words You Know
M T W Th F	Rounding Up the Rhymes
M T W Th F	Reading/Writing Rhymes
M T W Th F	Other _____

30 min.

Week of _____

Monday	
Tuesday	
Wednesday	
Thursday	
Friday	

Special Events This Week:

☐ **Guided Reading** `30-40 min.`

Before (5-10 min.)
During (15-20 min.)
After (5-10 min.)

M Before _____
   During _____
   After _____
T Before _____
   During _____
   After _____
W Before _____
   During _____
   After _____
Th Before _____
   During _____
   After _____
F Before _____
   During _____
   After _____

☐ **Self-Selected Reading** `30-40 min.`

Teacher Read-Aloud (5-10 min.)

M _____
T _____
W _____
Th _____
F _____

Reading Conferences (15-20 min.)

M _____
  _____
T _____
  _____
W _____
  _____
Th _____
  _____
F _____
  _____

Sharing (5-10 min.)

M _____
T _____
W _____
Th _____
F _____

☐ **Writing** `30-40 min.`

Mini-Lesson (5-10 min.)

M _____
T _____
W _____
Th _____
F _____

Writing/Conferences (15-20 min.)

M _____

T _____

W _____

Th _____

F _____

Sharing-Author's Chair (5-10 min.)

M _____
T _____
W _____
Th _____
F _____

☐ **Working with Words** `30 min.`

Word Wall Words (10 min.)

_____ _____
_____ _____
_____

On-The-Back Activity (See page 105)

M _____
T _____
W _____
Th _____
F _____

Words Activity (20 min.)
(Circle appropriate day)

M T W Th F   Making Words
M T W Th F   Guess the Covered Word
M T W Th F   Using Words You Know
M T W Th F   Rounding Up the Rhymes
M T W Th F   Reading/Writing Rhymes
M T W Th F   Other _____

Week of _____

Monday	
Tuesday	
Wednesday	
Thursday	
Friday	

Special Events This Week:

FOUR-BLOCKS WEEKLY RECORD

❐ Guided Reading

Before (5-10 min.)
During (15-20 min.)
After (5-10 min.)

30-40 min.

M Before _____
    During _____
    After _____

T Before _____
    During _____
    After _____

W Before _____
    During _____
    After _____

Th Before _____
    During _____
    After _____

F Before _____
    During _____
    After _____

❐ Self-Selected Reading

Teacher Read-Aloud (5-10 min.)

30-40 min.

M _____
T _____
W _____
Th _____
F _____

Reading Conferences (15-20 min.)

M _____

T _____

W _____

Th _____

F _____

Sharing (5-10 min.)

M _____
T _____
W _____
Th _____
F _____

❐ Writing

Mini-Lesson (5-10 min.)

30-40 min.

M _____
T _____
W _____
Th _____
F _____

Writing/Conferences (15-20 min.)

M _____

T _____

W _____

Th _____

F _____

Sharing-Author's Chair (5-10 min.)

M _____
T _____
W _____
Th _____
F _____

❐ Working with Words

Word Wall Words (10 min.)

30 min.

_____ _____

_____ _____

On-The-Back Activity (See page 105)

M _____
T _____
W _____
Th _____
F _____

Words Activity (20 min.)
(Circle appropriate day)

M T W Th F   Making Words
M T W Th F   Guess the Covered Word
M T W Th F   Using Words You Know
M T W Th F   Rounding Up the Rhymes
M T W Th F   Reading/Writing Rhymes
M T W Th F   Other _____

Week of _____

Monday		
Tuesday		
Wednesday		
Thursday		
Friday		

Special Events This Week:

❏ **Guided Reading** 🕐 30-40 min.

Before (5-10 min.)
During (15-20 min.)
After (5-10 min.)

M Before _____
During _____
After _____
T Before _____
During _____
After _____
W Before _____
During _____
After _____
Th Before _____
During _____
After _____
F Before _____
During _____
After _____

❏ **Self-Selected Reading** 🕐 30-40 min.

Teacher Read-Aloud (5-10 min.)

M _____
T _____
W _____
Th _____
F _____

Reading Conferences (15-20 min.)

M _____
_____
T _____
_____
W _____
_____
Th _____
_____
F _____
_____

Sharing (5-10 min.)

M _____
T _____
W _____
Th _____
F _____

❏ **Writing** 🕐 30-40 min.

Mini-Lesson (5-10 min.)

M _____
T _____
W _____
Th _____
F _____

Writing/Conferences (15-20 min.)

M _____
T _____
W _____
Th _____
F _____

Sharing-Author's Chair (5-10 min.)

M _____
T _____
W _____
Th _____
F _____

❏ **Working with Words** 🕐 30 min.

Word Wall Words (10 min.)

_____ _____
_____ _____

On-The-Back Activity (See page 105)

M _____
T _____
W _____
Th _____
F _____

Words Activity (20 min.)
(Circle appropriate day)

M T W Th F   Making Words
M T W Th F   Guess the Covered Word
M T W Th F   Using Words You Know
M T W Th F   Rounding Up the Rhymes
M T W Th F   Reading/Writing Rhymes
M T W Th F   Other _____

Week of _____

Monday	
Tuesday	
Wednesday	
Thursday	
Friday	

Special Events This Week:

FOUR-BLOCKS WEEKLY RECORD

❒ Guided Reading

30-40 min.

Before (5-10 min.)
During (15-20 min.)
After (5-10 min.)

M Before _____
   During _____
   After _____
T Before _____
   During _____
   After _____
W Before _____
   During _____
   After _____
Th Before _____
   During _____
   After _____
F Before _____
   During _____
   After _____

❒ Self-Selected Reading

30-40 min.

Teacher Read-Aloud (5-10 min.)

M _____
T _____
W _____
Th _____
F _____

Reading Conferences (15-20 min.)

M _____
T _____
W _____
Th _____
F _____

Sharing (5-10 min.)

M _____
T _____
W _____
Th _____
F _____

❒ Writing

30-40 min.

Mini-Lesson (5-10 min.)

M _____
T _____
W _____
Th _____
F _____

Writing/Conferences (15-20 min.)

M _____
T _____
W _____
Th _____
F _____

Sharing-Author's Chair (5-10 min.)

M _____
T _____
W _____
Th _____
F _____

❒ Working with Words

30 min.

Word Wall Words (10 min.)

_____
_____ _____
_____

On-The-Back Activity (See page 105)

M _____
T _____
W _____
Th _____
F _____

Words Activity (20 min.)
(Circle appropriate day)

M T W Th F   Making Words
M T W Th F   Guess the Covered Word
M T W Th F   Using Words You Know
M T W Th F   Rounding Up the Rhymes
M T W Th F   Reading/Writing Rhymes
M T W Th F   Other _____

Week of _____

Monday	
Tuesday	
Wednesday	
Thursday	
Friday	

Special Events This Week:

FOUR-BLOCKS WEEKLY RECORD

❏ Guided Reading

30-40 min.

Before (5-10 min.)
During (15-20 min.)
After (5-10 min.)

M Before _____
During _____
After _____

T Before _____
During _____
After _____

W Before _____
During _____
After _____

Th Before _____
During _____
After _____

F Before _____
During _____
After _____

❏ Self-Selected Reading

30-40 min.

Teacher Read-Aloud (5-10 min.)

M _____
T _____
W _____
Th _____
F _____

Reading Conferences (15-20 min.)

M _____
_____
T _____
_____
W _____
_____
Th _____
_____
F _____
_____

Sharing (5-10 min.)

M _____
T _____
W _____
Th _____
F _____

❏ Writing

30-40 min.

Mini-Lesson (5-10 min.)

M _____
T _____
W _____
Th _____
F _____

Writing/Conferences (15-20 min.)

M _____
_____
T _____
_____
W _____
_____
Th _____
_____
F _____
_____

Sharing-Author's Chair (5-10 min.)

M _____
T _____
W _____
Th _____
F _____

❏ Working with Words

30 min.

Word Wall Words (10 min.)

_____   _____
_____   _____
_____

On-The-Back Activity (See page 105)

M _____
T _____
W _____
Th _____
F _____

Words Activity (20 min.)
(Circle appropriate day)

M T W Th F   Making Words
M T W Th F   Guess the Covered Word
M T W Th F   Using Words You Know
M T W Th F   Rounding Up the Rhymes
M T W Th F   Reading/Writing Rhymes
M T W Th F   Other _____

Week of _____

Monday	
Tuesday	
Wednesday	
Thursday	
Friday	

Special Events This Week:

FOUR-BLOCKS WEEKLY RECORD

❏ Guided Reading

Before (5-10 min.)
During (15-20 min.)
After (5-10 min.)

30-40 min.

M Before _____
During _____
After _____

T Before _____
During _____
After _____

W Before _____
During _____
After _____

Th Before _____
During _____
After _____

F Before _____
During _____
After _____

❏ Self-Selected Reading

Teacher Read-Aloud (5-10 min.)

30-40 min.

M _____
T _____
W _____
Th _____
F _____

Reading Conferences (15-20 min.)

M _____

T _____

W _____

Th _____

F _____

Sharing (5-10 min.)

M _____
T _____
W _____
Th _____
F _____

❏ Writing

Mini-Lesson (5-10 min.)

30-40 min.

M _____
T _____
W _____
Th _____
F _____

Writing/Conferences (15-20 min.)

M _____

T _____

W _____

Th _____

F _____

Sharing-Author's Chair (5-10 min.)

M _____
T _____
W _____
Th _____
F _____

❏ Working with Words

Word Wall Words (10 min.)

30 min.

_____ _____

_____ _____

On-The-Back Activity (See page 105)

M _____
T _____
W _____
Th _____
F _____

Words Activity (20 min.)
(Circle appropriate day)

M T W Th F   Making Words
M T W Th F   Guess the Covered Word
M T W Th F   Using Words You Know
M T W Th F   Rounding Up the Rhymes
M T W Th F   Reading/Writing Rhymes
M T W Th F   Other _____

SELF-SELECTED READING

Teacher Read-Aloud (5-10 min.)

The teacher reads aloud to the class from a wide variety of materials. Ideas for read-alouds include:

- Fables
- Plays
- Fairy Tales
- Newspapers
- Magazines
- Easy Chapter Books
- Chapter Books
- Poetry
- Fiction
- Nonfiction

Independent Reading and Reading Conferences (15-20 min.)

The teacher holds individual conferences with the students scheduled for that particular day of the week, usually 3-5 students. The reading conference provides one-on-one, individual time afforded to students throughout the day. While the conferences take place, the remaining students in the class continue to read independently from materials in the reading area or the book baskets at their desks. The place where a conference occurs can vary.

- You may wish to go to the area where the student is reading and hold the conference there.
- You may wish to sit at a table and call each student over for the conference.

Sharing (optional) (5-10 min.)

Sharing variations might include:

- Reader's Chair.
- Using a microphone to "broadcast" a book talk.
- Talking from behind a "TV" screen replica.
- Reading a favorite book to younger students in the school.

Information appears in The Teacher's Guide to the Four Blocks®.

Reading Conference Questions

Teacher-Directed Conferences

First, most teachers ask each child to read a page or two from his chosen book to make sure that the child is reading "on level."

The teacher may then ask a general question or two:

- Why did you choose this book?
- Have you read any other book by this author? Which one?
- Is your book a fiction (made-up) book or nonfiction (informational) book? How can you tell?
- What do you think will happen next? Why do you think that?
- How did the author make the facts interesting in this book? Show me an example.

The teacher also encourages the student to look at reading from a writer's point of view:

- How did the author let you know that the main character was scared?
- Why was the beach a good setting for the story?
- If you had written this story, would you have chosen the same setting? Why or why not?
- Did you learn anything from this book that you can use in your own writing? If so, what?

If students have been working on a particular comprehension skill during Guided Reading, the teacher may ask questions that help the child apply these skills to the book he's chosen:

- Who are the characters?
- What is the setting?
- Was there a problem and did it get solved?
- Can you tell me what happened at the beginning, middle, and end of your story?
- What new facts did you learn from this book?
- This book has wonderful pictures of real places. Tell me about the pictures and what you learned from the pictures.
- Can you explain this chart about the parts of the animal's body to me?
- Can you read the map and explain where he traveled?

Child-Run Conferences

All children like to tell "what they think!" In child-run conferences, the student chooses the book and the pages in the book to share. The child tells why he picked the book, what he liked about it, etc. **Some open-ended questions to help students get started in forming opinions and telling about their reading preferences are listed below:**

- Do you like this book? Why or why not?
- What did you like about this book?
- What didn't you like about this book?
- What was your favorite part?
- Who was your favorite character? Why?
- Did the book have any pictures you really liked? Which one(s)?
- What was the most interesting thing you learned in this book?
- What was the funniest (saddest, most surprising, silliest, strangest) part of this book?

As the year progresses and children become fluent readers, there is more discussion and less reading aloud during the conference time. With fluent readers, reading aloud is used mostly to support the discussion. Assessment plays a small role in child-run conferences, but should not be the major focus.

Variations in Conference Focus

Occasionally, the teacher may want to help children anticipate the focus of the conference. In a classroom where a teacher has been stressing a certain skill or strategy during the Guided Reading or Writing Block, the teacher may say to the students, "We've been studying this week about how important the setting can be to a story. When you bring your book to share with me this week, let's talk about the setting of your book and whether it's important to the story."

She may want to remind them, "If you're reading an informational book, you probably won't have a setting because that's something writers include in telling a story, rather than when they write informational books."

Variations in how first graders read...

- They can "pretend read" by telling a story they know well in their own words.

- They can "picture read" a book with lots of illustrations by talking about the pictures.

- They can read by "reading all the words" when the story does not have too many words or words they do not know.

Information appears in *The Teacher's Guide to the Four Blocks®.*

Balance in Book Baskets

The Self-Selected Reading Block is multilevel in several ways. This block provides students the opportunity to choose and experience many different book genres while it helps to develop and support their interests and personal preferences.

The levels of books contained in the baskets and in other reading centers in the room should accommodate the range of independent reading levels within the class. There should be some "easy reads," many grade-level reading titles, and some challenging, above grade-level selections.

Some types of books to include in the book baskets: Fables, Fairy Tales, Plays, Nonfiction/Informational Books, Chapter Books, Biographies, Social Studies Connections, Science Connections, and Math Connections.

Use the reproducible at right to record the titles of books, magazines, and other materials you place in the baskets.

Balance in Book Baskets

_____
Date

Fables
_____
_____

Fairy Tales
_____
_____

Plays
_____
_____

Poetry
_____
_____

Nonfiction
_____
_____

Chapter Books
_____
_____

Social Studies Connections
_____
_____

Science Connections
_____
_____

Math Connections
_____
_____

Magazines
_____
_____

Other _____

Bookmarks

Enhance your students reading experience with bookmarks on page 96.

- **Duplicate and use the bookmarks to encourage children to read to and with their parents and then to discuss what they have read.**

- **Duplicate and use bookmarks to reinforce story elements such as important characters, time frame, setting, etc.**

- **Duplicate and use the "Reserved" bookmark for students to earmark books they want to read next.**

Reproducible bookmarks for use with the Self-Selected Reading activities are included on page 96. If you wish, enlarge the bookmarks for younger students or for students who have large handwriting.

Let's Read This Together!

Let's talk about

- the part we liked best...

- something new we learned...

- a character we will remember...

- whether we would read this book again...

Listen to Me Read This!

Once upon a time...

Let's talk about how

- I'm learning new words...

- I use the pictures to help figure out a word I don't know...

Please Read This to Me!

Once upon a time...

Let's talk about why

- I'm interested in learning more about this...

- I like books by this author...

Questions to Ask When

Reading together,

Being read to, or

Reading to someone

- What did you like best?
- What was funny? sad? surprising?
- What else would you like to know?
- What new words did you meet?

VIP Characters

Who's Who in

_____
Book Title

by

_____
Author

Character Names:

_____

I know they are VIP's because of...

- what they did (page where it happened)
- what they said (page where they said it)
- clues from the illustrations (page where illustration appears)
- what others said to or about them (page where it was said)

VIP Time Frame

_____
Book Title

_____
Author

This story takes place...
- in the present (today)
- in the past
- in the future

I know because...
- the pictures or illustrations show things that belong to...
- the character's dress gives clues...
- the names of places or people...

VIP Setting/Place

_____
Book Title

_____
Author

This story takes place...

_____

_____

The setting may include...
- a building, zoo, or farm
- a city, state, or country

I know the setting from...
- what the author says in the story.
- what the characters say.
- what I see in the illustrations.

RESERVED

_____
(Student's Name)

has reserved

_____
(Book Title)

by _____
(Author)

to read next.

_____
(Today's Date)

GUIDED READING

Before Reading (5-10 min.)

- Building/accessing prior knowledge
- Connecting to personal experiences
- Developing vocabulary
- Taking a "picture walk"
- Making predictions
- Setting purposes for reading
- Graphic organizer/KWL chart

During Reading (15-20 min.)

- Choral reading
- Echo reading
- Shared reading
- Partner reading
- Small, flexible groups
- Three-Ring Circus—reading alone, with partners, or with the teacher
- Book club groups
- ERT (Everyone-Read-To)
- Sticky Note reading

After Reading (5-10 min.)

- Discussing text/literature
- Connecting new and prior knowledge
- Following up predictions
- Acting out the story
- Discussing what they learned
- Discussing using reading strategies
- Completing graphic organizers or KWL chart

Before Reading

Picture Walks

The teacher guides students through a story using the pictures to develop concepts and vocabulary. The teacher asks questions to put the language of the text in the ears of the readers, such as

- "Do you know what this is called?" (pointing to an object in the picture)
- "What does it look like this character is doing?"
- "Can you tell in what season this story is taking place?"
- "Can you find where it says that word in the text?"
- "Who is that in the picture? Check the text on this page to see if you are right."

Picture Walks should...

- Be brief.
- Help students connect story concepts to their own experiences.
- Connect vocabulary to what is in the picture.
- Help readers anticipate and predict what will come next.
- Have readers dip into the text on some pages to match picture concepts and words.
- Introduce words that would be too difficult for many readers to figure out independently.
- Provide an overview of the story concept.

Before Reading

KWL's

KWL is an effective way to...

- **Help students use their prior knowledge base.**
- **Make predictions before beginning to read.**

A three-column chart headed with "What We Know," "Want to Learn," and "What We Learned" serves as the graphic organizer.

Directions for KWL charts:

- Ask what students know about the topic and record the information in the "What We Know" column.
- Ask what students would like to learn and record questions in the "Want to Learn" column.
- Ask students to see if they can find answers to the questions, confirm or disprove information under the "What We Know" column, or add interesting facts under "What We Learned."
- After reading is completed, gather the class around the KWL chart and respond to the three columns.

Animal Tracks		
Know	Want to Learn	Learned
Birds make tracks.	Do all animals make tracks?	
Animals make tracks.		
People can make tracks.	How can you tell which animal has left the tracks?	
Tracks are made by the feet or paws of animals.		
Different animals leave different kinds of tracks.		
Big animals make big tracks.		
Small animals make small tracks.		

Information appears in *The Teacher's Guide to the Four Blocks™*.

My Story Map

Name of story/book _____

Author _____

Setting: **When**   **Where**

Characters: **Who**

Problem:
  Beginning
  Middle
  End

Conclusion:

Story maps are effective ways to...
- Help students think about important story elements, like setting, characters, and plot.
- Help students learn about story events and sequence—beginning, middle, and end.

Directions for Story Maps:
- Discuss the content of the graphic organizer with students prior to reading the book.
- As students finish reading, ask them to make notes on information that goes on the map.

Information appears in *The Teacher's Guide to the Four Blocks®*.

Story Webs

Webbing is an effective way to...

- Help students organize information as they read.
- Help students categorize main ideas and related details.

This technique can be used with both fiction and nonfiction titles and is appropriate for students at any age. It is effective as an individual, partner, small group, or whole class activity.

Directions for Story Web:

- List the main topic of the book or reading selection in the large center circle.
- Spokes lead from the large center circle to smaller circles where different categories of details can be added.
- From each smaller circle, spokes lead to specific, related details or facts.

Webbing is a "before reading" activity when it requires students to access their prior knowledge base. It becomes a "during reading" activity when students locate and record facts while reading and add them to the web. Webbing is an "after reading" activity when the students share new facts, summarize information, and fill in the web after reading the book.

Information appears in *The Teacher's Guide to the Four Blocks®*.

Story Web

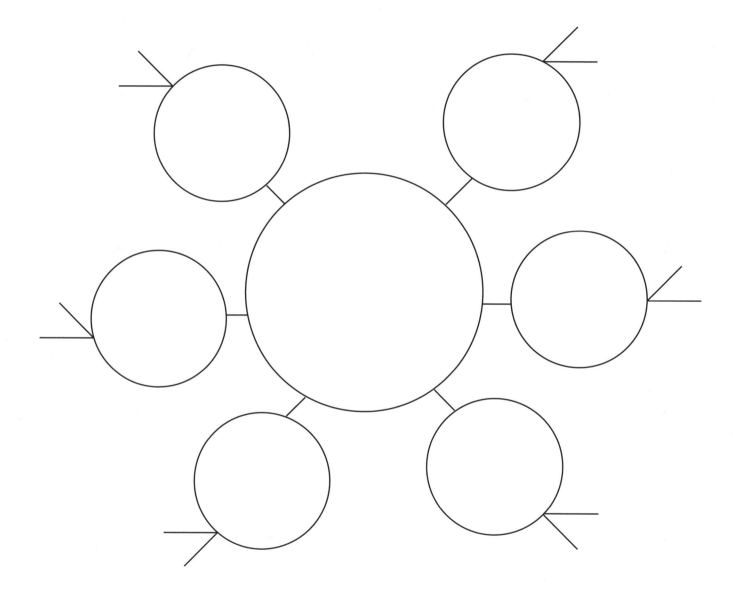

Everyone Read To (ERT)

ERT is a way of guiding reading when...

- Students are reading new text on their own.
- Keeping students together to provide guidance and support on initial reading.

Directions for Everyone Read To...

- Prior to ERT, the teacher and students read the title, examine the cover, discuss the author's and illustrator's names, and take a picture walk through the book.
- The teacher tells students how much to read and guides them through each two-page spread, reminding them of what they learned from the pictures and setting a purpose for their reading, such as "Everyone Read To find out more about the characters in the story."
- The purpose should be the "natural thing" students would want to find out after having seen and discussed the story during the picture walk.
- Students read the text for themselves in whatever way is appropriate. Older children usually read silently to themselves; emergent readers, who don't yet have the reading fluency to read it in their minds, "whisper" read.
- After students have read the selected text, the teacher follows up on whatever purpose was set for the reading.
- Using their own words, students share what they read with the group.
- Everyone proceeds to the next reading segment.
- The teacher might conclude the lesson by inviting emergent readers to "do the book" by acting out the story.

Sticky Note Reading

Sticky Note Reading can be done by individuals, partners, small groups, and by the whole class. Students use sticky notes to mark areas in the text.

Sticky Notes can be used to mark...

- What students find interesting.
- What students find important.
- What students find confusing.
- What proves or disproves students' earlier predictions.
- Words students do not know the meanings of or can't pronounce.

Once students know how to use sticky notes to mark information and troublesome words, you may give them two colors of sticky notes. For example, the students could use yellow notes to mark words or phrases that give information and pink notes for confusing words.

Students usually have more ideas to share during after-reading discussions when they have marked information with sticky notes as they encountered it.

Information appears in The Teacher's Guide to the Four Blocks®.

Partner Reading

Partner reading allows friends to help each other read.

Variations in Partner Reading...

- On "take turn days," partners alternate being the reader and help each other as needed.
- On "ask question days," partners read each page silently and ask each other questions about it before going on to the next page.
- On "sticky note days," partners have just a few sticky notes to mark things they want to remember as important, interesting, confusing, etc.
- Occasionally, the teacher may declare a "you decide day" when partners can decide to read together using any method they wish.

Tips for Assigning Partners...

- Pair students who work well together.
- Pair the most struggling readers with the most considerate and nurturing stronger readers.
- Give stronger readers a square shape in some colors, and those who will need more help a circle shape in the same colors. Have the students pair up by matching colors. The child with the square shape reads the first two pages where names and important vocabulary are usually introduced.

During Reading
Coaching Groups and Strategies

The teacher meets with a small, flexible group of students to coach them as they are reading. This coaching group is how the teacher helps students apply the strategies they have been learning. Students who need more support come to coaching groups more often.

Remind students of the strategies they can use to figure out an unknown word...

- Put your finger on the unknown word and say all the letters
- Use the letters in the word and the picture clues.
- Check the word to see if it contains a spelling pattern that you know.
- Think of a word that contains those letters and would make sense in the sentence.
- Keep your finger on the word and read the rest of the sentence to see if what you think the word is really does make sense.
- If your guess does not make sense, go back to the word and think of what else would make sense and have those letters.

Sample Coaching Statements...

- This word is spelled g-r-u-m-p. We have a Word Wall word spelled j-u-m-p. Use "jump" to help you read "grump."
- Do you see an animal in the picture that might be spelled d-i-n-o-s-a-u-r?
- What could you dig a hole with that begins with the "sh" sound?

Once the student has figured out what the unknown word is, remind him to go back and reread the sentence to see if it sounds right.

During and After Reading
Graphic Organizers

During reading, add any new information, facts, or details to the graphic organizers you started before reading. As an after reading activity, go back to the graphic organizers and fill in any missing information and summarize what you discovered in your reading.

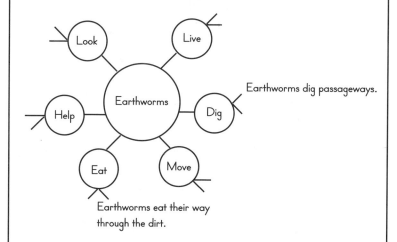

Earthworms dig passageways.

Earthworms eat their way through the dirt.

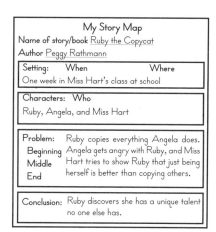

My Story Map
Name of story/book Ruby the Copycat
Author Peggy Rathmann

Setting: When   Where
One week in Miss Hart's class at school

Characters: Who
Ruby, Angela, and Miss Hart

Problem: Ruby copies everything Angela does.
Beginning   Angela gets angry with Ruby, and Miss
Middle   Hart tries to show Ruby that just being
End   herself is better than copying others.

Conclusion: Ruby discovers she has a unique talent
no one else has.

Reproducible graphic organizers for use with the Guided Reading activities are included on pages 98-99.

Information appears in *The Teacher's Guide to the Four Blocks®*.

After Reading
"Doing" the Book

Acting out the story is one of the best comprehension strategies because it integrates many story elements—characters, settings, actions, and sequence of events. This activity is done more often in grades K-1; retelling the story is usually done in grades 2-3. (Refer to pages 73-74 in *The Teacher's Guide to the Four Blocks™* by Patricia M. Cunningham, Dorothy P. Hall, and Cheryl M. Sigmon for more information on doing this activity with second and third graders.)

Good stories for acting out are those that...

- **Have between 5-8 characters.**
- **Have characters that keep reappearing in the story.**
- **Have repetitive phrases that are easy to remember.**
- **Have a strong story line.**

Book Titles: _____

_____

_____

_____

_____

_____

Mini-Lesson—Teacher Writing (5-10 min.)

- Teacher models real writing, a skill, or strategy on chart paper or on an overhead transparency.
- Mini-Lessons focus on writing, adding to, or editing a piece.
- Teacher refers to the Word Wall and other sources of words to help with spelling.
- Teacher models use of Editor's Checklist to promote and guide self-checking, peer revision, and editing.

Children Writing and Conferencing (15-20 min.)

- Students write on self-generated topics, individually paced at various stages of the writing process.
- As students write, the teacher holds individual editing conferences where students select a first draft to revise, edit, and finally publish.

Sharing (5-10 min.)

- Author's Chair—A few students each day share something they have written with the rest of the class (approximately two minutes for each child). The "author" answers several questions from classmates about the writing. The teacher models the types of thoughtful questions students should learn to ask each other.

Information appears in The Teacher's Guide to the Four Blocks®.

Variations in How Children Write in Primary Grades...

Variations in the Writing Block depend upon the time of the year and the grade level...

- **"Driting"**

  Early in the first grade, the Writing Block begins with "driting," a combination of drawing along with some circle/line/letter-like forms, some actual letters, a few words (sometimes copied from a book, sign, or calendar), and often a few numbers.

- **Half-and-Half Format**

  When most students in first grade are using both words and drawings in their "driting," it is time to move to paper with drawing space on the top half and lines for writing on the bottom half. This format may be a starting place for second or third graders with little writing experience. Because the paper is divided, it signals for the students the separation of writing from drawing. Some students like to draw first because the picture helps them organize their thoughts for writing. Other students prefer to write first and then draw the parts that can be portrayed in an illustration.

- **Writing, Revising/Editing, and Publishing**

  Students can now choose the paper (whether plain, half-and-half, or traditional handwriting paper) that will help them tell their story best. At this stage, students are writing on their own. Teachers are able to hold editing conferences with individual students.

Mini-Lesson

Topic: What to do when you can't spell a word

Strategies for spelling in a rough draft include...

- Check the Word Wall.
- Think about a word you can spell that rhymes with that word.
- Check charts around the room for reference.
- Stretch the word out, listen for the sounds, write down the letters the sounds represent.
- Circle the word and check it later.
- Save looking up a word in the dictionary for the editing stage.

Dear Jane,

Today I went for a walk near the train (traks) with my mom. We took a (snak) with us and had a (piknik) It was fun.

Love,
Susan

Rough Draft

---

*"**Black** is a Word Wall word. If black is spelled bl-ack, then track is probably spelled tr-ack, and snack is probably spelled sn-ack."*

Dear Jane,

Today I went for a walk near the train tracks with my mom. We took a snack with us and had a picnic. It was fun.

Love,
Susan

Final Draft

Editing Checklist: Capitalization and Punctuation

If language skills are to transfer to writing, they must be taught during writing. To help your students grasp these important skills, develop and gradually add to an editing checklist for punctuation, capitalization, and grammar. As students self-check their rough drafts, they put a check mark at the bottom of their page of writing as they check for each criteria listed.

Editing Checklist
1. Name and date
2. Sentences make sense
3. Ending punctuation . ? !
4. Beginning capitals
5. Capitals for names
6. Circle possible misspellings
7. Title in center
8. Stays on topic

After introducing each of the items on the checklist and as students' writing matures, give each student in your class an editing checklist to keep at his desk by copying the reproducible shown at right.

Information appears in *The Teacher's Guide to the Four Blocks®*.

Editing Checklist
1. Name and date
2. Sentences make sense
3. Ending punctuation . ? !
4. Beginning capitals
5. Capitals for names
6. Circle possible misspellings
7. Title in center
8. Stays on topic

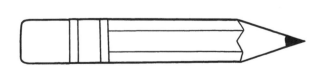
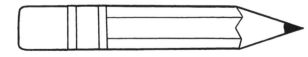

Writing Conferences

The writing conference allows teachers to work one-on-one with students to choose, revise, and edit one good piece of their writing.

During the writing conference, the teacher may want to make notes about the strengths and weaknesses of a student's writing. The teacher might focus on the following questions as she works with each student.

Writing Conferences Checklist

Student's Name: _____

Date: _____

Check all that apply:

❑ **Understands the concept of staying focused in his writing.**

❑ **Uses simple punctuation correctly (period, exclamation point, question mark).**

❑ **Uses the Word Wall and other resources in the room during writing.**

❑ **Has a sense of what a sentence is.**

❑ **Generates different topics on her own.**

❑ **Needs additional assistance in where to get ideas about what to write.**

❑ **Uses the Editor's Checklist for a quick edit after writing a rough draft.**

❑ **Demonstrates a basic understanding of phonics.**

❑ **Understands the concept of words and letters as demonstrated by the spacing between words and letters.**

❑ **Works independently to develop a piece of writing over several days.**

❑ **Needs to be encouraged to extend a piece of writing over several days.**

❑ **Demonstrates more confidence in his writing.**

Focused Writing Weeks

The teacher models the writing process for students during mini-lessons. She "thinks aloud" as she writes and talks about what she is doing and why. The teacher leads students through each step in the writing process.

1. **Brainstorming**

   The teacher tells the students to choose topics they know a lot about for their writing. He demonstrates how they can narrow down several ideas to one topic. The students may also use a story map or web to help organize their thoughts before they begin writing.

2. **First (Rough) Draft**

   The teacher leads students through the process of writing a good first draft that can later be edited and revised. She explains that since they will eventually share their writing with the class, their work must be correct.

3. **Revising**

   The teacher helps the students polish their writing. He may put the children into small groups and have each child read her work to the others in the group. The group members then tell the author something they liked, ask questions, and offer any suggestions for making the writing better.

4. **Editing**

   The children refer to the editing checklist their teacher has gone over and displayed in the classroom. They read their work for each item on the checklist and decide what needs to be changed. When the students finish editing, they sometimes do peer editing, then they share their drafts with the teacher in a final editing conference.

5. **Final Copy (Publishing)**

   The students use their best handwriting to copy over their edited work. The teacher may display the students' stories on a bulletin board or bind them together to create a class book.

Author's Chair

The Writing Block ends with the Author's Chair, in which several students each day share first drafts or a published piece. It is a time when children can listen to what their peers are writing. What children read in the Author's Chair gives the other children in the class new ideas for their writing. The students reading their pieces also get a chance to show off their writing skills.

The same sharing variations used in the Self-Selected Reading Block may also be used for students sharing their writing in the Author's Chair...

- Let children speak into a microphone to read their written pieces. Inexpensive microphones seem to "bring out the ham" in kids and help them project their voices so that everyone can hear them.

- Create a cardboard replica of a large TV screen and let students share their work from behind the screen. Most children love being a TV star!

- Throw an "author party" one afternoon every two or three weeks. Students' names are pulled from a jar, and they form groups of three or four in which everyone gets to share his writing. Author parties, like other parties, often include refreshments such as popcorn or cookies. Children develop all kinds of tasty associations with writing and sharing!

One way teachers can assure that the Writing Block is a successful experience for all levels of writers is to spend a minute or two with a struggling reader before that child shares his work in the Author's Chair. If the child wants to share from a first-draft piece but is unable to read it, and if the teacher can't read it either, the teacher will coach the child to "tell" his piece rather than read it. If a struggling reader is about to read from a published piece for which the teacher has provided a lot of help, the teacher will practice read it with the child a time or two to assure that he can read it fluently when he is in the Author's Chair.

Information appears in *The Teacher's Guide to the Four Blocks®* and *Implementing the 4-Blocks® Model.*

Word Wall (Daily) (10 min.)

- Add words gradually (5 per week).
- Choose a location for the Word Wall that is accessible.
- Make sure the words are large enough to be easily read from anywhere in the room.
- Practice words daily by chanting and writing them.
- Do On-the-Back activities involving the words.
- Hold students accountable for spelling Word Wall words correctly in any writing they do.

Decoding/Spelling Activity (20 min.)

Choose one of these activities to do in addition to the Word Wall each day.

- Making Words
- Guess the Covered Word
- Using Words You Know
- Rounding Up the Rhymes
- Reading and Writing Rhymes
- Tongue Twisters

Information appears in *The Teacher's Guide to the Four Blocks®*.

On-the-Back Activities

These activities expand on Word Wall word applications. They should be included when the Word Wall activity (chanting and writing the words) can be completed in five minutes, thus leaving five minutes for this activity.

On-the-Back Activities can focus on skills such as...

- **Adding endings to Word Wall words**
- **Rhyming Words**
- **Be A Mind Reader riddles**

Adding Endings to Word Wall Words

The following is a sample lesson to demonstrate this activity:

The teacher might say, "Today, we are going to work on how to spell these Word Wall words (eat, talk, jump, look, and play) when they need an ending. Listen to the sentences, find the Word Wall word, and decide how to spell the word with the ending."

Sentences: I love <u>eating</u> hamburgers.

Who is <u>talking</u> to the teacher?

All of the girls are having fun <u>jumping</u> rope.

LaDawn <u>looked</u> in many stores for some new clothes.

Andre <u>plays</u> ball with Kevin at recess.

Be A Mind Reader

Be A Mind Reader is a Word Wall review activity that can also be used as an On-the-Back activity. To do this as an On-the-Back activity, the teacher selects a Word Wall word without telling the students what it is. She gives the students five clues and asks them to see if they can "read her mind" and guess what the word is.

The following is a sample lesson to demonstrate this activity:

If the Word Wall word that has been selected is "talk," then the teacher might give the following clues:

1. It's one of the words on the wall.

2. It has four letters.

3. It has an "a" in it.

4. It begins with "t."

5. It rhymes with "walk."

First Grade Word Wall Words

after	he	said
all	her	saw
am	here	school
and	him	see
animal	his	she
are	house	sister
at	how	some
be	I	talk
best	in	teacher
because	is	tell
big	it	that
boy	jump	the
brother	kick	them
but	like	there
can	little	they
can't	look	thing
car	made	this
children	make	to
come	me	up
day	my	us
did	new	very
do	nice	want
down	night	was
eat	no	we
favorite	not	went
for	of	what
friend	off	when
from	old	where
fun	on	who
get	out	why
girl	over	will
give	people	with
go	play	won't
good	pretty	you
had	quit	your
has	rain	zoo
have	ride	

Second Grade Word Wall Words

about	into	slow
after	it's	small
again	joke	snap
are	jump	sometimes
beautiful	junk	sports
because	kicked	stop
before	knew	tell
best	line	than
black	little	thank
boy	made	that's
brothers	mail	their
bug	make	them
can't	many	then
car	more	there
caught	name	they
children	new	they're
city	nice	thing
clock	not	those
could	off	to
crash	one	too
crashes	or	trip
didn't	other	truck
don't	our	two
drink	outside	use
eating	people	very
every	phone	wanted
favorite	played	was
first	pretty	went
float	quit	were
found	rain	what
friends	really	when
girl	ride	where
green	right	who
gym	said	why
have	sale	will
here	saw	with
house	school	won
how	shook	won't
hurt	sister	write
I	skate	writing

Third Grade Word Wall Words

about	hole	there
again	hopeless	they
almost	I'm	they're
also	impossible	thought
always	independent	threw
another	into	through
anyone	it's	to
are	its	too
beautiful	journal	trouble
because	knew	two
before	know	unhappiness
buy	laughed	until
by	let's	usually
can't	lovable	vacation
city	myself	very
could	new	want
community	no	was
confusion	off	wear
countries	one	weather
didn't	our	we're
discover	people	went
doesn't	pretty	were
don't	prettier	what
enough	prettiest	when
especially	probably	where
everybody	question	whether
everything	really	who
except	recycle	whole
exciting	right	winner
favorite	said	with
first	school	won
friendly	something	won't
getting	sometimes	wouldn't
general	terrible	write
governor	that's	your
have	their	you're
hidden	then	

Making Words

 Making Words is an active, hands-on manipulative activity in which children learn to look for patterns in words and learn how changing just one letter in a word can create a new word.

To begin the Making Words activity:

Select a word for the Making Words lesson. Give each students the letter cards needed to spell out the word. Place the same letters on index cards in a pocket chart in the front of the room.

Make Step:

- For first graders only, begin the lesson by telling the students that every word must have a vowel and then tell them what today's vowel is.
- Write the number of letters in the word on the board. The first word the students will make has this number of letters, and the students know that one of the letters is the vowel.
- Tell the students what the word is and use it in a sentence. Have the students say the word, stretch it out, and "make" the word on their desktops.
- Let one student make the word in the pocket chart as the rest of the class checks to see if their words are made correctly.
- Place an index card with the word written on it in the pocket chart for later sorting.
- Add, rearrange, or take away letters from the word to change it into the next word in the lesson. Let a different student make the new word in the pocket chart while the class checks the words they have made. Write the new word on an index card and place it in the pocket chart for later sorting activities.
- Make and check all the words the same way.

Sort Step:

- Direct students' attention to the words on index cards which will now be sorted.
- Ask the students to find all the words that begin with a particular letter.
- Ask students to find any words that rhyme.
- Ask students to find all words that have a particular spelling pattern or ending.

Transfer Step:

- Tell students that they will meet other words in their reading that have some of the same spelling patterns and endings as the words they are learning now. If they can remember how to spell these words, then they can figure out new words that have similar spellings.
- Tell students that thinking of a known rhyming word will help them spell a new word if they want to use the new word in their writing.

Information appears in *The Teacher's Guide to the Four Blocks®* and *Month-By-Month Phonics for Third Grade.*

Sample Lesson 1

Mystery word: plans

Letters: a, l, n, p, s

Make: an, pan, nap, lap, slap, snap, plan, plans

Sort: words that start with *s*, words that start with *p*, words that rhyme with *an*, and words that rhyme with *ap*.

Transfer: man, cap, map, tan

Sample Lesson 2

Mystery word: rabbits

Letters: a, i, b, b, r, s, t

Make: at, sat, rat, bat, bar, tar, star, stir, stair, rabbits

Sort: words that start with *b*, words that start with *st*, words that rhyme with *at*, and words that rhyme with *ar*.

Transfer: that, flat, jar, scar

Sample Lesson 3

Mystery word: community

Letters: i, o, u, c, m, m, n, t, y

Make: not, cot, cut, nut, mom, Tom, into, city, tiny, unity, mount, count, county, mutiny, community

Sort: words that end with *y* and words that rhyme.

Transfer: prom, plot, strut, clot

Guess the Covered Word

When students meet an unknown word while **Guess the covered word.** reading, they need to know how to use consonant and context clues as a cross-checking strategy. In every grade level, Guess the Covered Word is first taught with the covered word at the end of the sentence, then gradually progresses to the covered word in the middle of the sentence, and finally, with the covered word(s) located within a paragraph.

Strategy for Guess the Covered Word:

Ask yourself...

- What word makes sense in this sentence?
- Is this a long or a short word?
- What letter(s) does the word begin with and what are all the other letters in the word?

To begin the Guess the Covered Word activity:

Write several sentences on the board or on a piece of chart paper. Cover the word to be guessed with two sticky notes. The first sticky note should cover the onset (all the letters before the first vowel). The other sticky note should cover the rime (the rest of the word).

The sticky notes should be cut to fit the size of the word exactly, no bigger. Making the size of the sticky notes correspond to the size of the word allows students to use word length as a clue.

The sentences chosen for this activity can use math, science, social studies, literature, or theme content.

Steps for the Guess the Covered Word activity:

- Read the sentence and record 3 or 4 guesses for the covered word.
- Remove the first sticky note. Cross out any guesses that don't begin with the correct letter(s). If none of the guesses fit, record additional guesses that make sense and start with the letter(s).
- Uncover the rest of the word. Check all the letters and see if a guess from the list was correct.

First Grade Lesson

At School

Doris likes to <u>read</u>.

Akiko likes to do <u>math</u>.

Joyce likes to <u>write</u>.

Philemon likes to draw pictures with <u>markers</u>.

Juan likes to play <u>basketball</u>.

Second Grade Lesson

Fall

In the fall, <u>most</u> leaves change colors.

Some are red, yellow, and <u>orange</u>.

They <u>float</u> slowly to the ground.

Colorful leaves cover sidewalks and <u>driveways</u>.

I help my dad <u>clean</u> up the leaves.

Third Grade Lesson

At the Fair

Every fall, my family spends a <u>weekend</u> enjoying the fair. Rides like the ferris wheel and the <u>carousel</u> are our favorites. Eating delicious, freshly baked <u>pizza</u> at the fair has become a family tradition. We also play games and buy <u>souvenirs</u>.

In the examples above, the word to be covered is indicated by underlining.

Changing a Hen to a Fox

Early in the year, it's good to assess how much students know about beginning and ending consonants and vowel sounds. The following example provides a fun way to check out how much students know. (For additional "Changing a Hen to a Fox" lessons, refer to pages 45-46 in *Month-By-Month Phonics for Second Grade* by Dorothy P. Hall and Patricia M. Cunningham.)

Write the word "hen" on the board so the class can easily copy it. Ask the students if they can change a "hen" to a "fox."

Change **hen** to **pen**.
Change **pen** to **pet**.
Change **pet** to **pit**.
Change **pit** to **sit**.
Change **sit** to **six**.
Change **six** to **fix**.
Change **fix** to **fox**.

With each step, give the students clues about how to reach the next word in the sequence. For example, after writing "hen" on the board, spell the word for the students and have them repeat the spelling back to you. You may want to say something like, "Now that we know that h-e-n spells hen, what letter can we change to make it spell pen? What letter does the word pen begin with?" and so on. Do this for each step until you reach the end. Your students have now successfully changed a hen to a fox!

Information appears in *The Teacher's Guide to the Four Blocks®* and *Month-By-Month Phonics for Second Grade*.

Rounding Up the Rhymes

Rounding Up the Rhymes is a great activity to follow the reading of a selection during Guided Reading (or a book the teacher has read aloud at Self-Selected Reading time) which has several pages on which there are rhyming words with the same spelling pattern. Using the rhymes from a book and doing some transfer rhymes increases the probability that children will actually use rhyming words they know as they encounter new words in their reading and writing. Rounding Up the Rhymes is appropriate to do when most students in the class have developed the ability to hear rhymes and are ready to see how rhyming patterns work.

Steps to Rounding Up the Rhymes:

Read the book:

- Reread several pages of the selected book, focusing on the rhyming words. Encourage the students to chime in and try to hear the rhymes.

Round Up the Rhymes:

- As students pick out rhyming words, write them on index cards and place in a pocket chart.
- Remind students that words which rhyme usually have the same spelling pattern. (Discard any rhyming words which do not have the same spelling pattern.) Have students go to the pocket chart and underline the spelling pattern in each set of rhymes.

Transfer step:

- The students will use the rhyming words to read and write other words they may not have seen before. For the reading transfer, write a few new words, and let students decide which words with the same spelling pattern will help them to read the new words. Without pronouncing the new words, choose students to place the new words in the pocket chart with the rhyming words that match them. For the spelling transfer, pronounce the new words and let students decide with which words they rhyme, then ask students to use the rhymes to spell the new words. At the end, the rounded-up rhymes and the transfer words will be lined up in the pocket chart.

© Carson-Dellosa CD-8206

Reading/Writing Rhymes

Reading and Writing Rhymes is an activity which gives students practice using patterns to decode and spell lots of other words.

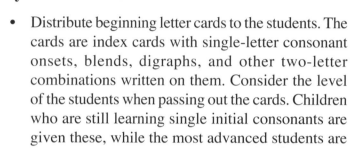

Steps to Reading/Writing Rhymes:

- Distribute beginning letter cards to the students. The cards are index cards with single-letter consonant onsets, blends, digraphs, and other two-letter combinations written on them. Consider the level of the students when passing out the cards. Children who are still learning single initial consonants are given these, while the most advanced students are given the less-common, more complex onsets.

- Write the spelling pattern with which the class is working (ex. __ap) eight times on a piece of chart paper. Have the children help spell and pronounce the pattern.

- Invite students to come up who have onset cards that they think will make words (gap, chap, snap, etc.) Have the student place the card next to one of the written spelling patterns and pronounce the word. If the word is a real word, use the word in a sentence and write that word on the chart. (If the word is not a real word, do not write it on the chart.)

- Once the chart of rhyming words is written, write a silly rhyme with the class using lots of the rhyming words.

- Then, have the students write rhymes of their own. You may want to put students in small groups or with partners to write the rhymes, then let different children read their rhymes to the class.

Below are some of the most common rhyming patterns for short vowel sounds to use in Reading/Writing Rhymes:

a:	ack	ad	am	ap	ash	at	an	and
e:	ed	et	est	ell	en			
i:	ick	id	ip	ill	it	in		
o:	op	ot	ock	ob				
u:	uck	ug	ump	unk	ut	unch		

Tongue Twisters

Tongue Twisters are a fun way for students to review consonants, blends, and digraphs because there is such a concentration of words with the same beginning sound so close together.

Steps for doing Tongue Twisters:

- Read the Tongue Twister to the class and have them repeat it, both quickly and slowly, focusing attention on the beginning sound.

- Write a Tongue Twister on the board or on a piece of chart paper and have students focus attention on the beginning letters (in print).

- Have students read the Tongue Twister with you.

- Students can illustrate Tongue Twisters, or if you use a Tongue Twister from a book that has been illustrated, you may want to let students search the illustration to find as many items as possible that begin with the sound on which you are focusing.

Refer to page 110 for Tongue Twister examples.

Information appears in *The Teacher's Guide to the Four Blocks®*.

Tongue Twisters for Beginning Consonants and Vowels:

Andrew admitted his answer was absolutely accurate.

Carl's camera captures colors coming from Carol's casual calico costume.

Cassidy carries cauliflower, carrots, and corn in her colorful cart.

Danny digs deep in his pockets to find dirt, a dime, and a dollar.

Hope handed hungry Henry a handful of hamburgers.

Logan likes limes, lettuce, lemons, and lots of licorice.

Pam put a pack of pencils, a pad of paper, a pot of paste, and a palette of paint on the table.

Peter and Paul paste purple paper pelicans on pink paper.

Regan remembers radishes, red roses, ripe raspberries, and raisins.

Susan successfully searches for some books about the Sun and Saturn.

Tongue Twisters for Blends and Digraphs:

Bruce's brother brought broccoli in brown boxes.

Brenda brings brown bran bread to Brian for breakfast.

Children like chewing chocolates, cheese, chicken, and cherries.

The crawling crab crossed a crate of cranberries.

Grady, the grouchy grocer, grew some green grapes, grapefruit, and grains.

Placido places plenty of plants on a plastic plate.

Scott the scarecrow scares away the scavenging crows with his scarf.

Shelby shares shirts, shorts, and shoes with Shea.

Parent/Guardian Contact Record

Student _____ Date _____

Parent/Guardian _____

Teacher _____

❑ **Phone Call**   ❑ **Fax**
❑ **Note Home**   ❑ **E-mail**
❑ **Conference**

Focus: _____

_____

_____

Content: _____

_____

_____

Follow-Up/Action: _____

_____

_____

Long Term Planning

January	February	March	Notes
April	May	June	
July	August	September	
October	November	December	

2006

January
S	M	T	W	T	F	S
1	2	3	4	5	6	7
8	9	10	11	12	13	14
15	16	17	18	19	20	21
22	23	24	25	26	27	28
29	30	31				

February
S	M	T	W	T	F	S
			1	2	3	4
5	6	7	8	9	10	11
12	13	14	15	16	17	18
19	20	21	22	23	24	25
26	27	28				

March
S	M	T	W	T	F	S
			1	2	3	4
5	6	7	8	9	10	11
12	13	14	15	16	17	18
19	20	21	22	23	24	25
26	27	28	29	30	31	

April
S	M	T	W	T	F	S
						1
2	3	4	5	6	7	8
9	10	11	12	13	14	15
16	17	18	19	20	21	22
23	24	25	26	27	28	29
30						

May
S	M	T	W	T	F	S
	1	2	3	4	5	6
7	8	9	10	11	12	13
14	15	16	17	18	19	20
21	22	23	24	25	26	27
28	29	30	31			

June
S	M	T	W	T	F	S
				1	2	3
4	5	6	7	8	9	10
11	12	13	14	15	16	17
18	19	20	21	22	23	24
25	26	27	28	29	30	

July
S	M	T	W	T	F	S
						1
2	3	4	5	6	7	8
9	10	11	12	13	14	15
16	17	18	19	20	21	22
23	24	25	26	27	28	29
30	31					

August
S	M	T	W	T	F	S
		1	2	3	4	5
6	7	8	9	10	11	12
13	14	15	16	17	18	19
20	21	22	23	24	25	26
27	28	29	30	31		

September
S	M	T	W	T	F	S
					1	2
3	4	5	6	7	8	9
10	11	12	13	14	15	16
17	18	19	20	21	22	23
24	25	26	27	28	29	30

October
S	M	T	W	T	F	S
1	2	3	4	5	6	7
8	9	10	11	12	13	14
15	16	17	18	19	20	21
22	23	24	25	26	27	28
29	30	31				

November
S	M	T	W	T	F	S
			1	2	3	4
5	6	7	8	9	10	11
12	13	14	15	16	17	18
19	20	21	22	23	24	25
26	27	28	29	30		

December
S	M	T	W	T	F	S
					1	2
3	4	5	6	7	8	9
10	11	12	13	14	15	16
17	18	19	20	21	22	23
24	25	26	27	28	29	30
31						

2007

January
S	M	T	W	T	F	S
	1	2	3	4	5	6
7	8	9	10	11	12	13
14	15	16	17	18	19	20
21	22	23	24	25	26	27
28	29	30	31			

February
S	M	T	W	T	F	S
				1	2	3
4	5	6	7	8	9	10
11	12	13	14	15	16	17
18	19	20	21	22	23	24
25	26	27	28			

March
S	M	T	W	T	F	S
				1	2	3
4	5	6	7	8	9	10
11	12	13	14	15	16	17
18	19	20	21	22	23	24
25	26	27	28	29	30	31

April
S	M	T	W	T	F	S
1	2	3	4	5	6	7
8	9	10	11	12	13	14
15	16	17	18	19	20	21
22	23	24	25	26	27	28
29	30					

May
S	M	T	W	T	F	S
		1	2	3	4	5
6	7	8	9	10	11	12
13	14	15	16	17	18	19
20	21	22	23	24	25	26
27	28	29	30	31		

June
S	M	T	W	T	F	S
					1	2
3	4	5	6	7	8	9
10	11	12	13	14	15	16
17	18	19	20	21	22	23
24	25	26	27	28	29	30

July
S	M	T	W	T	F	S
1	2	3	4	5	6	7
8	9	10	11	12	13	14
15	16	17	18	19	20	21
22	23	24	25	26	27	28
29	30	31				

August
S	M	T	W	T	F	S
			1	2	3	4
5	6	7	8	9	10	11
12	13	14	15	16	17	18
19	20	21	22	23	24	25
26	27	28	29	30	31	

September
S	M	T	W	T	F	S
						1
2	3	4	5	6	7	8
9	10	11	12	13	14	15
16	17	18	19	20	21	22
23	24	25	26	27	28	29
30						

October
S	M	T	W	T	F	S
	1	2	3	4	5	6
7	8	9	10	11	12	13
14	15	16	17	18	19	20
21	22	23	24	25	26	27
28	29	30	31			

November
S	M	T	W	T	F	S
				1	2	3
4	5	6	7	8	9	10
11	12	13	14	15	16	17
18	19	20	21	22	23	24
25	26	27	28	29	30	

December
S	M	T	W	T	F	S
						1
2	3	4	5	6	7	8
9	10	11	12	13	14	15
16	17	18	19	20	21	22
23	24	25	26	27	28	29
30	31					

2008

January
S	M	T	W	T	F	S
		1	2	3	4	5
6	7	8	9	10	11	12
13	14	15	16	17	18	19
20	21	22	23	24	25	26
27	28	29	30	31		

February
S	M	T	W	T	F	S
					1	2
3	4	5	6	7	8	9
10	11	12	13	14	15	16
17	18	19	20	21	22	23
24	25	26	27	28	29	

March
S	M	T	W	T	F	S
						1
2	3	4	5	6	7	8
9	10	11	12	13	14	15
16	17	18	19	20	21	22
23	24	25	26	27	28	29
30	31					

April
S	M	T	W	T	F	S
		1	2	3	4	5
6	7	8	9	10	11	12
13	14	15	16	17	18	19
20	21	22	23	24	25	26
27	28	29	30			

May
S	M	T	W	T	F	S
				1	2	3
4	5	6	7	8	9	10
11	12	13	14	15	16	17
18	19	20	21	22	23	24
25	26	27	28	29	30	31

June
S	M	T	W	T	F	S
1	2	3	4	5	6	7
8	9	10	11	12	13	14
15	16	17	18	19	20	21
22	23	24	25	26	27	28
29	30					

July
S	M	T	W	T	F	S
		1	2	3	4	5
6	7	8	9	10	11	12
13	14	15	16	17	18	19
20	21	22	23	24	25	26
27	28	29	30	31		

August
S	M	T	W	T	F	S
					1	2
3	4	5	6	7	8	9
10	11	12	13	14	15	16
17	18	19	20	21	22	23
24	25	26	27	28	29	30
31						

September
S	M	T	W	T	F	S
	1	2	3	4	5	6
7	8	9	10	11	12	13
14	15	16	17	18	19	20
21	22	23	24	25	26	27
28	29	30				

October
S	M	T	W	T	F	S
			1	2	3	4
5	6	7	8	9	10	11
12	13	14	15	16	17	18
19	20	21	22	23	24	25
26	27	28	29	30	31	

November
S	M	T	W	T	F	S
						1
2	3	4	5	6	7	8
9	10	11	12	13	14	15
16	17	18	19	20	21	22
23	24	25	26	27	28	29
30						

December
S	M	T	W	T	F	S
	1	2	3	4	5	6
7	8	9	10	11	12	13
14	15	16	17	18	19	20
21	22	23	24	25	26	27
28	29	30	31			

2009

January
S	M	T	W	T	F	S
				1	2	3
4	5	6	7	8	9	10
11	12	13	14	15	16	17
18	19	20	21	22	23	24
25	26	27	28	29	30	31

February
S	M	T	W	T	F	S
1	2	3	4	5	6	7
8	9	10	11	12	13	14
15	16	17	18	19	20	21
22	23	24	25	26	27	28

March
S	M	T	W	T	F	S
1	2	3	4	5	6	7
8	9	10	11	12	13	14
15	16	17	18	19	20	21
22	23	24	25	26	27	28
29	30	31				

April
S	M	T	W	T	F	S
			1	2	3	4
5	6	7	8	9	10	11
12	13	14	15	16	17	18
19	20	21	22	23	24	25
26	27	28	29	30		

May
S	M	T	W	T	F	S
					1	2
3	4	5	6	7	8	9
10	11	12	13	14	15	16
17	18	19	20	21	22	23
24	25	26	27	28	29	30
31						

June
S	M	T	W	T	F	S
	1	2	3	4	5	6
7	8	9	10	11	12	13
14	15	16	17	18	19	20
21	22	23	24	25	26	27
28	29	30				

July
S	M	T	W	T	F	S
			1	2	3	4
5	6	7	8	9	10	11
12	13	14	15	16	17	18
19	20	21	22	23	24	25
26	27	28	29	30	31	

August
S	M	T	W	T	F	S
						1
2	3	4	5	6	7	8
9	10	11	12	13	14	15
16	17	18	19	20	21	22
23	24	25	26	27	28	29
30	31					

September
S	M	T	W	T	F	S
		1	2	3	4	5
6	7	8	9	10	11	12
13	14	15	16	17	18	19
20	21	22	23	24	25	26
27	28	29	30			

October
S	M	T	W	T	F	S
				1	2	3
4	5	6	7	8	9	10
11	12	13	14	15	16	17
18	19	20	21	22	23	24
25	26	27	28	29	30	31

November
S	M	T	W	T	F	S
1	2	3	4	5	6	7
8	9	10	11	12	13	14
15	16	17	18	19	20	21
22	23	24	25	26	27	28
29	30					

December
S	M	T	W	T	F	S
		1	2	3	4	5
6	7	8	9	10	11	12
13	14	15	16	17	18	19
20	21	22	23	24	25	26
27	28	29	30	31		